VOLUME 13 •

MW01113449

GREAT COMMISSION
RESEARCH JOURNAL

Published by the Great Commission Research Network

Published by the Great Commission Research Network (GCRN)
GCRN's Registered Agent: Corporation Service Company
7716 Old Canton Road, Suite C
Madison, MS 39110

www.greatcommissionresearch.com

Printed in the United States of America by Martel Press, Claremont, CA

Correspondence: 695 E. Bougainvillea St., Azusa, CA 91702 USA

THE PURPOSE of the *Great Commission Research Journal* is to communicate recent thinking and research related to effective church growth and evangelism.

THE JOURNAL The *Great Commission Research Journal* (formerly, *The Journal of the American Society for Church Growth*) is published semi-annually, Fall and Spring. It is indexed in *Religious and Theological Abstracts, Christian Periodical Index*, and the *Index to Book Reviews in Religion, Religion Indexes: Ten Year Subset of CD-ROM*.

ISSN 1947-5837 (print)
ISSN 2638-9983 (online)
ISBN 978-0-9986175-8-9

THE OPINIONS AND CONCLUSIONS published in the Great Commission Research Journal are solely those of the individual authors and do not necessarily represent the position of the Great Commission Research Network.

CONTENTS

Editorial

Articles

Book Reviews

GREAT COMMISSION
RESEARCH JOURNAL
2021, Vol. 13(1) 5-18

The Importance of Hypotheses in Church-Based Research

David R. Dunaetz, Editor

Abstract

The role of hypotheses is central both in church-related research and in Christian ministry. Hypotheses guide the collection of data to determine what is true in research and provide tentative guidelines for action in ministry, even when they are not yet confirmed. Well-constructed hypotheses are based on previous research and provide clear potential solutions to research problems. They succinctly posit a testable relationship between two or more variables. Such hypotheses can be tested through appropriately designed research. Statistical techniques can indicate to what degree the evidence collected supports the hypotheses. In church-based research, hypotheses to be examined can come from a body of literature (e.g., the Church Growth Movement), a practitioner's experience, theories from other domains (e.g., the Social Brain Hypothesis; Dunbar, 1993), and modeling phenomena using analogies (e.g., modeling the church lifecycle as an epidemic; Hayward, 2015, 2018).

The Importance of Hypotheses in Church-Based Research

Church-based research is not simply collecting data and discovering what it says. If we have access to data from churches, it is most likely that the data provided does not record all the information that could be useful in understanding what is happening in the churches. Certainly, if we have specific questions that we are trying to answer, such as "What elements of worship are most effective for evangelism?", "How do church members understand baptism?", or "Do fundamentalist churches have a more authoritarian structure than non-fundamentalist churches?", very specific information will need to be collected. To ensure that the appropriate data is collected, researchers propose specific hypotheses that will guide the research design so that the data collected can be analyzed in such a way that will lead to some type of conclusion concerning the truth of these hypotheses.

Sometimes hypotheses are not the beginning of research design (as is typical in quantitative research) but are the results of research (which is common in qualitative research). When researchers seek to initially understand a phenomenon, they may collect data from several examples or interview various people who have first-hand knowledge of this phenomenon and then make subjective conclusions or hypotheses about the phenomenon. Such an approach has been common in much church-based research focusing on effective evangelism and church planting (McGavran, 1955; Moon, 2020; Wagner, 1989). However, the hypotheses proposed in such qualitative studies are often tentative. More rigorous quantitative studies testing of these hypotheses can find stronger evidence to support them, or the studies can find that the additional evidence does not support them.

In order to form high-quality hypotheses for research and practice, let us examine some important concepts related to hypothesis creation.

Research Problems, Research Questions and Hypotheses

The best research provides solutions to problems that we face. In Great Commission-focused research, these problems typically concern understanding how to better obey and fulfill the Great Commission (Matt. 28:18-20) in various contexts. These problems may be quite general, such as the difficulties involved in bringing the gospel to and making disciples in closed countries (also known as creative access countries; Barnett, 2005), or they can be rather narrow, such as the difficulties that first-time attenders have in connecting with people at a megachurch. If we want to find a solution to these problems through research, these problems can be considered *research problems.* Clearly identifying the research problem enables us to focus our research and makes it more likely that a solution will be found. In our examples, the research problems might be phrased as "Missionaries are often ineffective in creative access countries" and "First-time visitors to American megachurches often leave without warm, personal interaction with church members, resulting in feeling that the church is cold and unwelcoming."

After we define the research problem, we need to find a *research question,* a question the response to which will help solve the research problem. The response might not completely solve the problem, but it should provide a partial solution that leads us to better understand what we can do to better address the problem. For a given research problem, the research question can be broad or narrow. For example, "How do effective missionaries (versus ineffective missionaries) share the gospel in creative-access countries?" and "Does having a large number of followers on local social media (versus fewer followers) lead to more opportunities to share the gospel in face-to-face situations for missionaries in creative-access countries?" are both useful research questions. The more narrow or specific the question is, the easier it will be to design appropriate research that will provide at least a partial solution to the research problem. For the problem concerning our example of first-time visitors at megachurches, we can use research questions such as "How have recently baptized church members (who did not know anyone in the church the first time they attended) met people and developed relationships?" or "Are visitors more likely to meet someone in megachurches that use individual seats or in the megachurches that use pews?"

Once the researcher has limited the scope of the research to a specific research question, the search for a testable *hypothesis* can begin. A hypothesis is a statement that, if true, provides at least a partial solution to the research problem. It is a statement that answers the research question or at least contributes to a partial answer. The following list (Dunaetz, 2020) provides some characteristics of a good hypothesis from a scientific point of view:

1. It is a response to a research question clearly expressed in a declarative statement.
2. It posits a relationship between two or more variables.
3. It reflects a theory or body of literature upon which it is based.
4. It is brief and to the point.
5. It is testable.

Since one of the principal reasons that we make hypotheses in research is to decide if it is supported by the evidence or not, the hypothesis needs to be expressed as a clear declaration of a potential fact that can be either supported or not supported by whatever data we collect. "First-time visitors meet lots of people in churches with chairs" is too vague for research purposes. "First-time visitors meet more people in churches with chairs than in churches with pews" is much clearer and more specific, making it more suitable for a research hypothesis.

Secondly, a good hypothesis needs to posit a relationship between two or more variables. A variable is anything that can be measured which can take on different values according to the context. In our example with pews and chairs, the first variable is the type of seating. In a study of 21st century American megachurches, chairs and pews might be the only types of seating that interest us. In other contexts, we might include standing or sitting on a rug as possible values that this variable can take on. For each church in our study, we would record the type of seating they have. The second variable would be the number of warm interactions that first-time visitors have. This would be a numeric value, perhaps typically between 0 and 5. This variable would be more difficult to measure than the type of seating in a church. We could develop some type of survey for first-time visitors to complete, or we could be more creative and study a high-resolution video recording of the audience before and after the service, assuming we would be able to identify who the first-time visitors were.

The third criteria for good research hypotheses is that the hypothesis is based on some theory or body of literature. There should be a theoretical reason that the hypothesis might be true. By having an idea of why something is true, we can better examine the precise conditions under which it will be true and better know how to adapt the hypothesis to other contexts. For example, the hypothesis concerning warm interactions and church seating is based partially on the concept of psychological safety (Baer & Frese, 2003; Edmondson & Lei, 2014), the degree to which a person feels safe in undertaking a risky behavior (such as introducing themselves to someone). Families or affinity groups typically may leave a greater distance between themselves and strangers in pews (perhaps 24 to 48 inches) than they do in chairs (typically one chair, typically with a width of 22-24 inches) because the undefined borders of personal space in pews makes sitting close less psychologically safe. It is likely to be easier and more natural to start a warm interaction with someone when they are within 24 inches from the initiator than when they are more distant, hence the chairs versus pews hypothesis.

The fourth criteria of a good research hypothesis is that it is brief and to the point. It is one thing to find evidence that supports a hypothesis which can contribute to fulfilling the Great Commission, but it is altogether different to propagate the conclusions and have people integrate them into their life and ministry. The more clearly and concisely the hypothesis and the resulting conclusions can be stated, the more likely they are to be accepted by a wide audience.

The final criteria is that the hypothesis needs to be testable. Unless we can collect data that provides evidence that a hypothesis is true or not, the hypothesis simply remains an educated guess. However, if we can test our hypothesis, and if there is strong evidence to support it, the hypothesis moves into the shared body of knowledge concerning a phenomenon, often called theory. For example, if data supported the hypothesis that first-time visitors to megachurches have more warm social interactions in churches with chairs rather than in churches with pews, the importance of using chairs would move more solidly into church growth theory.

Testing Hypotheses

But how would we actually test this hypothesis? This is where a hundred years of advances in statistics and the social sciences becomes very useful. Before the data is collected, the research needs to be designed carefully so that it is most likely to provide us with the data needed. For example, data from 1000 visitors in 30 megachurches (15 with chairs and 15 with pews) could provide the information needed. If the data indicates that the visitors had an average of 2.00 warm interactions in churches with chairs and 1.00 warm interactions in churches with pews, this would provide evidence that supports the hypothesis (these numbers are chosen for convenience; I suspect that they might be lower in some churches). The strength of the evidence would depend on the specific statistical approach and the validity of the research design.

We could simply say that 2.00 warm interactions in the churches with seats is greater than 1.00 warm interactions in the churches with pews, so we conclude that chairs are superior to pews. This is the simplest way to test a hypothesis. We look at the various options and decide which one the evidence points to. This might be the most common approach in qualitative research (Creswell & Poth, 2016; Patton, 2014) and theology (Lewis & Demarest, 1996). As always in research, this approach is heavily dependent on logic and the quality of the data available to the researcher. But this approach is also limited by human biases and heuristic thinking. When faced with ambiguous information, as Francis Bacon (1620/1902) said, we prefer to believe what we prefer to be true. The difference between 2.00 warm welcomes and 1.00 warm welcomes is pretty large, but if the two values were .80 warm welcomes and .70 warm welcomes, would we conclude that the difference is certain enough and large enough to justify the conclusion that chairs are better than pews?

To reduce some of the uncertainties associated with data, statisticians use the concept of *null hypothesis significance testing* (Fisher, 1925) to determine if we can be reasonably sure or not that the data supports a hypothesis. If we want to know if our research hypothesis is strongly supported by the data, we can look at the opposite of the hypothesis, which is known as the null hypothesis because it includes the possibility that the relationship that we seek to confirm does not exist. For example, if our hypothesis is "First-time visitors meet more people in churches with chairs than in churches with pews," then our null hypothesis would be "First-time visitors *do not* meet more people in churches with chairs than in churches with pews" or, its logical equivalent, "First-time visitors in churches with chairs meet *the same number or fewer* people in churches with pews."

The value of the null hypothesis is that it includes the idea that nothing happens because of the variable under consideration (e.g., the seating used by churches), that is, any differences are due to chance. Now, when things happen by chance, especially things related to human behavior, their outcomes are typically normally distributed, that is, their frequency is distributed as a bell curve. For example, if the average person meets 1.00 people, that means that quite often they meet 1 person, but sometimes 0 or 2 people; occasionally they might meet 3 people, but it would be very rare for them to meet 100 people. Statisticians have a very good understanding of what types of results we should expect if things happen by chance. This means that if we have data, we can calculate the probability of obtaining such data if it were simply due to chance (i.e., the null hypothesis is true). Scientists generally agree on the convention that when these probabilities are less than 5% (less than 1 chance out of 20), then we have strong evidence that the results did not happen by chance, that is, the null hypothesis is very likely not true. Now if the null hypothesis is not true, then, by logical necessity, our research hypothesis is true. Hence if the calculated probability of the data occurring by chance is less than 5% (i.e., $p <$

.05), then we have found strong objective evidence that our research hypothesis is true, and this despite any subjective biases that we might have. If $p < .05$, we say that the hypothesized relationship or difference is statistically significant, meaning that we have good reason to believe that it is true, and that the data is not the spurious result of chance.

When testing a hypothesis, we also need to consider whether it is a directional hypothesis (e.g., visitors will meet *more* people in churches with chairs than in churches with pews) or exploratory, also known as a non-directional hypothesis (e.g., visitors will meet *a different number* of people in churches with chairs than in churches with pews). Normally, we want to make a directional hypothesis; it is easier to reach statistical significance if we are only looking for a difference in one direction. Directional hypotheses are also known as one-tailed hypotheses because we're only looking for the probability of events happening by chance in one tail of the bell curve. However, if we are not sure of what direction the results are going to go (e.g., we have a theoretical reason that pews might be better than chairs as well as a theoretical reason that chairs might be better than pews), we should make the non-directional hypothesis that the number of people met in the two types of churches will be different. It is more difficult to reach statistical significance with this type of study (we have to look at both tails of the normal distribution), but if the data is statistically significant in either direction ($p < .05$), then we can make a conclusion about which of the two theories is better in our context.

The Origin of Hypotheses

Where do hypotheses come from? There is no limit to the source of hypotheses, but experience indicates that some routes are more fruitful than others. In the early days of the Church Growth Movement, many of the hypotheses came from the writings of Donald McGavran (McGavran, 1955; McGavran & Wagner, 1990) as described by Charles Arn (2021) in this issue of the *Great Commission Research Journal*. Other church growth hypotheses grew out of biblical concepts and the experiences of church consultants and practitioners (Arn, 1987; McIntosh, 1999, 2003; Moon, 2020).

Exploratory hypotheses can come from a synthesis of best practices and folk wisdom. Dunaetz and Priddy (2014) explored the veracity of truisms associated with church growth (such as "Churches that emphasize prayer grow faster than those which do not" or "Churches which emphasize foreign missions grow faster than those which do not.") by examining pastoral attitudes to determine what drove church growth. The results indicated some truisms were supported by the data, while others were not (e.g., prayer predicted church growth while emphasizing world missions did not.).

Other academic disciplines are also a rich source of hypotheses, often contributing to theory that provides causal explanations for church-based phenomena, rather than simply describing what is observed (Hayward, 1999). Hypotheses related to evangelism, discipleship, and church life can come from such fields as history (Hellerman, 2003), cultural psychology (Hunter, 1996), leadership theory (Lim, 2004), and psychology (Dunaetz et al., 2018). Reflections on contemporary events also serve as sources of hypotheses relevant to the Great Commission, such as the COVID-19 pandemic (Rainier, 2020) or, as in this issue of the journal, China's growing influence in the world (Lee, 2021).

Church-Related Hypotheses from the Social Brain Hypothesis

As the study of the growth of churches develops, the theory explaining the phenomena that have been observed grows as well. For example, Bretherton and Dunbar (2020) of the University of Lincoln (UK) have applied Dunbar's (1993) social brain hypothesis to the growth and functioning of churches. The social brain hypothesis states that human brains are limited to forming cohesive groups with a maximum size of approximately 150 members. Once a group grows much past 150, group cohesion decreases because we cannot have an especially meaningful relationship with everyone in the group due to our cognitive limitations. This provides a theoretical framework for understanding congregational growth and structure based on human brain capacity. It leads to several very specific hypotheses (Bretherton & Dunbar, 2020) describing phenomena that have been noted in church growth literature. *Member engagement and participation will be lower in larger churches than in smaller churches.* Because group cohesion is lower when churches are much larger than 150 people, there will be an increase in freeloading, with a relatively larger fringe group than in smaller churches. This phenomenon has long been observed in churches (Hussey, 2016; von der Ruhr & Daniels, 2012; Wicker, 1969; cf. Dunaetz, 2021).

Churches with more than 150 people need to have smaller groups. For members to feel that they are an important part of the group, typically groups of 150 or less are needed. The exact upper limit depends on the personality mix, the culture, and the social expectations of the group's members. Most churches are under the 150 person limit, so they can function as a cohesive whole (McIntosh, 1999). Larger churches, in contrast, often have extensive small group ministries to meet their members' needs for community (Hartwig et al., 2020; Wuthnow, 1994)

Churches will struggle with restructuring to grow beyond 150 people. In churches with less than 150 people, the church functions as a cohesive whole where everyone knows each other. However, this unified whole cannot exist if it continues to grow. Once a church reaches approximately 150 people, visitors and potential new members are less likely to be integrated into the community because the existing members have little ability to develop relationships with new people (George & Bird, 2017; Wagner, 1990). To continue growing, the church as a whole cannot be each member's primary social group. This will require some type of reorganization, typically with a second staff person added, that permits the creation of other entities that serve as primary social group; such reorganization can lead to struggles and conflict because existing members do not want to lose what they value.

Although these three hypotheses (Bretherton & Dunbar, 2020) describe well-documented phenomena, having a theoretical framework such as the social brain hypothesis (Dunbar, 1993) to understand why they occur provides a structure for developing more effective strategies to address the problems associated with the phenomena.

Creating Hypotheses with Analogies: Modeling the Church Lifecycle as an Epidemic

One approach to developing hypotheses is to look for similarities between an observed phenomenon (e.g., the growth and decline of churches) and a phenomenon in another domain (Wicker, 1985). It has long been observed that churches have life cycles, typically described by slow initial growth, followed by more rapid growth, plateauing, and then a gradual decline (Arn, 1985; Malphurs & Penfold, 2014; McIntosh, 2009; Moberg, 1962). John Hayward of the University of South Wales recognized that this cycle was similar to the spread of a pandemic and its eventual decline (Hayward, 1999, 2005). Using what we know about pandemics, he has developed a mathematical model that assumes that the gospel and conversions propagate like viruses and infections: A few people are very contagious, infect others, and gradually become less contagious, resulting in fewer infections. People eventually become immune or die off, resulting in a long slow decline of the number infected.

This model (Hayward, 1999, 2005) leads to a number of hypotheses that are not especially common in ministry-focused circles, but which might be true:

a. Conversion growth is highly correlated with contact between believers who are effective evangelists and non-believers.

b. People who are effective evangelists tend to be effective for a limited period of time.

c. A few people who are very effective in evangelism (super-spreaders) have a greater impact on the church than many people who are only mildly effective.

d. In populations with few Christians, initial church growth will be very slow.

e. When large parts of a population are Christians, periods of growth will not last long.

f. Church growth doesn't end because of secularisation, but because effective evangelists disappear or have no contact with non-Christians.

Such modeling and hypotheses permit us to think about evangelism, social networks, and spiritual gifting in ways that could lead to fruitful research and insights concerning effective ministry.

Conclusion

We have seen that hypotheses play an essential role in church-based research and practice. Clear statements concerning how behaviors, concepts, and other church-related phenomena relate to each other serve as a guide for future research, provide tentative guidelines for present ministry, and may be used as a tool for evaluating what we are currently doing and evaluating what we have done in the past. My prayer for all of the readers of the *Great Commission Research Journal* and for each member of the Great Commission Research Network is that they develop solid hypotheses which describe human behavior and responses in church-based ministry, that they collect data to evaluate whether they are true, and that they communicate their conclusions to others who can benefit from their research so that the Great Commission can be fulfilled in ever more effective ways.

David R. Dunaetz, General Editor

References

Arn, C. (2021). My pilgrimage in Church Growth. *Great Commission Research Journal, 13*(1), 61-85.

Arn, W. (1985). Is your church in a mid-life crisis? *The Win Arn Growth Report, 7*, 1-2.

Arn, W. (1987). *The Church Growth ratio book: How to have a revitalized, healthy, growing, church.* Church Growth, Inc.

Bacon, F. (1620/1902). *Novum organum* (J. Devey, Ed.). P. F. Collier & Son.

Baer, M., & Frese, M. (2003). Innovation is not enough: Climates for initiative and psychological safety, process innovations, and firm performance. *Journal of Organizational Behavior, 24*(1), 45-68.

Barnett, M. (2005). Creative access platforms: What are they and do we need them? *Evangelical Missions Quarterly, 41*(1), 88-96.

Bretherton, R., & Dunbar, R. I. M. (2020). Dunbar's number goes to church: The social brain hypothesis as a third strand in the study of church growth. *Archive for the Psychology of Religion, 42*(1), 63-76.

Creswell, J. W., & Poth, C. N. (2016). _Qualitative inquiry and research design: Choosing among five approaches._ Sage.

Dunaetz, D. R. (2020). _Research methods and survey applications: Outlines and activities from a Christian perspective_ (3rd ed.). Martel Press.

Dunaetz, D. R., Jung, H. L., & Lambert, S. S. (2018). Do larger churches tolerate pastoral narcissism more than smaller churches? _Great Commission Research Journal, 10_(1), 69-89.

Dunaetz, D. R., & Priddy, K. E. (2014). Pastoral attitudes that predict numerical Church Growth. _Great Commission Research Journal, 5,_ 241-256.

Dunaetz, D. R., Smyly, C., Fairley, C. M., & Heykoop, C. (2021). Values congruence and organizational commitment in churches: When do shared values matter? _Psychology of Religion and Spirituality,_ Advance online publication.

Dunbar, R. I. M. (1993). Coevolution of neocortical size, group size and language in humans. _Behavioral and Brain Sciences, 16_(4), 681-694.

Edmondson, A. C., & Lei, Z. (2014). Psychological safety: The history, renaissance, and future of an interpersonal construct. _Annual Review of Organanizational Psychology and Organizational Behavior, 1_(1), 23-43.

Fisher, R. A. (1925). _Statistical methods for research workers._ Oliver and Boyd.

George, C. F., & Bird, W. (2017). _How to break growth barriers: Revise your role, release your people, and capture overlooked opportunities for your church._ Baker Books.

Hartwig, R. T., Davis, C. W., & Sniff, J. A. (2020). _Leading small groups that thrive._ Zondervan.

Hayward, J. (1999). Mathematical modeling of church growth. _Journal of Mathematical Sociology, 23_(4), 255-292.

Hayward, J. (2005). A general model of church growth and decline. _Journal of Mathematical Sociology, 29_(3), 177-207.

Hellerman, J. H. (2003). When the church was family: Revisioning Christian community in light of ancient social values. _Great Commission Research Journal, 14_(3), 19-37.

Hunter, G. G., III. (1996). The rationale for a culturally relevant worship service. _Great Commission Research Journal, 7,_ 131-144.

Hussey, I. (2016). The big news on small churches: Re-evaluating the contribution of small churches to the fulfillment of the great commission. _Great Commission Research Journal, 7_(2), 172-183.

Lee, P. (2021). China's belt and road initiative: Mission opportunities and challenges. _Great Commission Research Journal, 13_(1), 19-37.

Lewis, G. R., & Demarest, B. A. (1996). _Integrative theology._ Zondervan.

Lim, D. S. (2004). Cho younggi's charismatic leadership and Church Growth. _Great Commission Research Journal, 15_(2), 3-28.

Malphurs, A. A., & Penfold, G. E. (2014). _Re:Vision: The key to transforming your church._ Baker.

McGavran, D. A. (1955). _The bridges of God: A study in the strategy of missions._ World Dominion Press.

McGavran, D. A., & Wagner, C. P. (1990). *Understanding Church Growth* (Third ed.). Eerdmans.

McIntosh, G. L. (1999). *One size doesn't fit all: Bringing out the best in any size church*. Revell.

McIntosh, G. L. (2003). *Biblical church growth: How you can work with God to build a faithful church*. Baker Books.

McIntosh, G. L. (2009). *Taking your church to the next level: What got you here won't get you there*. Baker Books.

Moberg, D. O. (1962). *The church as a social institution: The sociology of American religion*. Prentice-Hall.

Moon, W. J. (2020). Alternative financial models for churches and church plants: When tithes and offerings are not enough. *Great Commission Research Journal, 12*(1), 19-42.

Patton, M. Q. (2014). *Qualitative research & evaluation methods: Integrating theory and practice* (4th, Ed.). Sage Publications.

Rainier, T. S. (2020). *The post-quarantine church: Six urgent challenges and opportunities that will determine the future of your congregation*. Tyndale Momentum.

von der Ruhr, M., & Daniels, J. P. (2012). Examining megachurch growth: Free riding, fit, and faith. *International Journal of Social Economics, 39*(5), 357-372.

Wagner, C. P. (1989). *Strategies for church growth: Tools for effective mission and evangelism*. Wipf and Stock Publishers.

Wagner, C. P. (1990). *Church planting for a greater harvest: A comprehensive guide*. Regal Books.

Wicker, A. W. (1969). Size of church membership and members' support of church behavior settings. *Journal of Personality and Social Psychology, 13*(3), 278.

Wicker, A. W. (1985). Getting out of our conceptual ruts: Strategies for expanding conceptual frameworks. *American Psychologist, 40*(10), 1094-1103.

Wuthnow, R. (1994). *Sharing the journey: Support groups and America's new quest for community*. Simon and Schuster.

GREAT COMMISSION
RESEARCH JOURNAL
2021, Vol. 13(1) 19-37

China's Belt and Road Initiative: Mission Opportunities and Challenges

Paul Lee

Abstract

The Belt and Road Initiative (BRI) is an infrastructure project proposed by China to improve transportation in Eurasia. This will bring both mission opportunities and challenges in the regions affected. God is perhaps giving Christians a unique opportunity for evangelism through this project which facilitates the movement of not just humans and products, but also the gospel.

Mainland China adopted a capitalist economic system in 1979, thirty years after adopting a communist political system. The country joined the World Trade Organization (WTO) in 2001. The Gross Domestic Product (GDP) surged from less than US$ 150 billion in 1978 to more than US$ 8.3 trillion in 2012 (Purdy, 2013). China has a high-speed railway network of 26,869 kilometers, a system longer than that of all the other countries in the world combined (Nunno, 2018). The globalization of production and the availability of inexpensive labor has caused China to be considered the world's factory (Lu, 2019). The production of construction materials has been particularly successful in China. This production is consistently higher than China's internal utilization and is continually increasing; concrete production increased from 450 million tons in 2008 to 2.4 billion tons in 2017 (McCarthy, 2018). Apart from the simple need for economic development, this success concerning the production of construction materials has led to economic pressure to increase exports and undertake foreign building projects.

The Belt and Road Initiative (BRI), in Chinese, 一帶一路 (literally One-Belt-One-Road), is an economic, diplomatic, and cultural exchange plan that was proposed by the Chinese national leader Xi Jinping in 2013 (Ministry of Foreign Affairs, 2013). The "Belt" is a land-based "Silk Road Economic Belt" (絲綢之路經濟帶), named after to the land-based transportation network between China and the Middle East during the Han Dynasty (206BC to 220AD). The "Road" is the sea-based "Maritime Silk Road of the 21st Century" (21世紀海上絲綢之路) with allusions to the seven sailing voyages of the Chinese sea captain Zheng He from China to Africa in the 13th century. The initiative integrates both the land and maritime infrastructure to form a mega-logistic network in Eurasia.

The Belt aspect of the project focuses on building a network of six transcontinental high-speed railway and highway networks from China to Central Asia and Europe (Lim *et al.*, 2016). These six land routes (Figure 1) are tentatively:

1. Beijing (China) – Ulaanbaatar (Mongolia) – Moscow (Russia)
2. The New Eurasian Land Bridge (the refitting of eight international freight rail routes to no longer require a break-of-gauge)
3. Urumqi (China) – Tashkent (Uzbekistan) – Istanbul (Turkey)
4. Kashgar (China) – Gwadar (Pakistan)
5. Bangladesh–China–India–Myanmar
6. Kunming (China) – Thailand and Vietnam – Malaysia – Singapore.

The annual exchange of goods and people along the routes will increase substantially. Natural resources, such as methane and metal ores from the Central Asian countries, including Kazakhstan,

Kyrgyzstan, Tajikistan, Uzbekistan, Turkmenistan, and Ukraine, will be exported to China more readily. In the other direction, China can export manufactured goods and construction materials to these countries. The international trade among these countries will substantially increase.

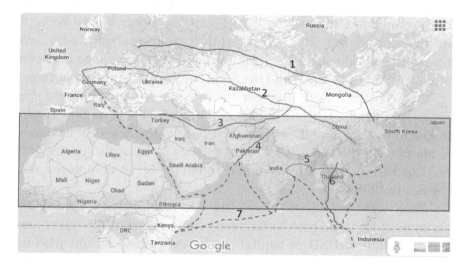

Figure 1. *Combined map of the 10/40 Window and the Belt-and-Road Initiative. The framed rectangle is the 10/40 window. Solid lines numbered 1 to 6 are the routes of the Silk Road Economic Belt. The blue dotted line number 7 is the 21st century Maritime Silk Road system. The dotted line under the rectangle is the equator from Google Maps software.*

The Road refers to the development of the maritime infrastructure (Figure 1). From Fujian Province, off the coast of Taiwan, the Chinese government will work with local governments to build ports, container terminals, and local land roads to expedite the loading, unloading, and transportation of containers. Also known as the 21st Century Maritime Silk Road, this project focuses on the southern provinces of China along the South China Sea and China's main trade partners in Southeast Asia, including Indonesia, Vietnam, and Singapore. From Singapore, the routes pass through the Strait of Malacca westward to the Indian Ocean to India, Sri Lanka, and Kenya in East Africa. China has leased many seaports around the Indian Ocean for periods ranging from 10 to 99 years.

From East Africa, trade can be brought to the Mediterranean via the Suez Canal. Trade with the West can then utilize a land route again from Italy, with a focus on reaching Rotterdam, the largest seaport in Europe. The South China Sea trade already contributes 1.4 trillion USD per year of trade for China versus 208 billion USD per year of trade with the USA (Center for Strategic Studies, 2017). China would like to diversify the options for connecting to Eastern Asia, Africa, and the West, rather than relying only on transportation through the Strait of Malacca (the passage between Malaysia and Indonesia) and the South China Sea. Another purpose of the Maritime Silk Road is to provide a shorter route for petroleum products from the Middle East, first to Gwadar port in Pakistan by ship, and then by highway and railway within Pakistan to southwestern China. This route will be significantly shorter and less costly than the current route through the Strait of Malacca and the South China Sea.

Sixty-eight countries along the BRI routes have signed an agreement to participate in financing these projects. A total of one hundred billion USD of capital stock and twenty billion paid-in capital were guaranteed. The overall monetary pool will be managed by the Asian Infrastructure Investment Bank (AIIB; AIIB, 2020). The AIIB and the government of the People's Republic of China have signed an agreement on taxes, legal status, and operations. (AIIB Agreements, 2015). The AIIB also has Memorandums of Understanding on cooperation and co-financing with 1) the African Development Bank, 2) the African Development Fund, 3) the Asian Development Bank, 4) the European Bank for Reconstruction and Development, 5) the Eurasian Development Bank, 6) the European Investment Bank, 7) the Inter-American Development Bank and Inter-American Investment Corporation, 8) the Islamic Development Bank Group, 9) the New Development Bank, and 10) the World Bank Group (AIIB Partnership, 2019). The AIIB also partners with private financial institutions and cooperates with other partners in the public and non-governmental sectors (Wang, 2014). The presidency of the AIIB will rotate among the member states. The board of directors vote on the approval of projects. This multilateral development bank is responsible for providing the capital to fund the infrastructure projects in BRI.

The Missiological Significance of the Belt-and-Road-Initiative

In terms of strategy for world missions, one can observe that the BRI network overlaps with many countries in the 10/40 Window map (Figure 1). This means that the BRI may be the transportation network that God uses to spread the gospel to unreached peoples who have never been exposed to the gospel. Although air travel is faster than railway and sea route, it is inferior to the latter in terms of cost and its capacity to transport people and goods. This multi-hub network designed to support the industrial supply chain may be exactly the infrastructure needed to evangelize unreached peoples in many of the countries of the 10/40 Window.

The BRI requires a very large investment of capital. Although the most economically able, the United States has chosen not to invest in Eurasia's infrastructure through this initiative. China, being the second greatest economic force in the world, has been building bilateral relationships with countries in Asia and Europe to gain their support. Although China's economic growth seems to make the country able to complete this project, such growth may not be sustainable and the ability to bring to fruition the entire project is not certain. Whatever the infrastructure which is developed, it may not provide access to all the countries of the 10/40 Window, but some doors may be opened by it, permitting Christians to enter countries that may not stay open forever.

The BRI will increase globalization as more people and goods travel across the continents. Not only will there be goods and services exchanged, but the flow of humans will also lead to a substantial exchange of culture, beliefs, and worldviews. This phenomenon has been common in the West but will grow exponentially along the routes of the BRI. The presence of Africans in China (Marsh, 2014) or Chinese workers throughout Africa (Nunoo, 2014) will become a common phenomenon. As such international exchange increases, one can envision that these open doors will permit the sending of long-term missionaries and the support of local Christian workers to Unengaged Unreached People

Groups (UUPGs) along the BRI route, although creativity may still be needed to take advantage of these opportunities. Nevertheless, the goal of bringing the gospel to all UUPGs will be within reach more than ever before.

The Mission Opportunities Along the Belt-And-Road Countries

The speed and breadth of gospel sharing may increase in the 10/40 Window countries due to the ability of Christians to enter them via the BRI infrastructure. The recent political persecution of Christians in China has been forcing Chinese Christians to leave China and seek asylum in other countries (Farr, 2019), similar to the persecution of believers in Jerusalem described in Acts 8. If such persecution continues in China, those who leave via the BRI will have every opportunity to share the gospel with the people in the countries where they settle. They will join missionaries who have been sent out by Chinese house churches, including those sent in the context of the Back to Jerusalem movement (Park, 2015; Stafford, 2004), some of whom have been blocked from returning home due to political reasons. As the church grows along the BRI, these new churches will be among peoples who are culturally close to the remaining unreached. Discipleship ministries will enable them to evangelize more effectively and rapidly members of UUPGs to whom they are culturally near.

Many countries along the BRI do not grant visas to traditional missionaries. Therefore, to send evangelists and church planters to these countries, churches and organizations must figure out other platforms or legal means to obtain entry visas or long-term visas from the country of interest. Entering these Creative Access Nations (Wei, *et al.*, 2016) will require Christians to take on secular jobs, using tentmaking, business-as-Missions, or bi-vocational models of ministry. These jobs may be with either traditional for-profit companies or nonprofit Non-Government Organizations (NGOs) which provide relief and social services.

For-profit companies focused on eco-tourism (Kaarieni & Tuah, 2019) or hospitality management may be excellent platforms due to the expected growth of these sectors. The BRI infrastructure will attract tourists to previously inaccessible regions. Restaurants and hotels can be developed that preserve the local environment and meet the needs of travelers. Eco-tourism not only improves the local economy but educates the community concerning the importance of protecting the environment.

The need for medical providers, such as doctors, dentists, nurses, and pharmacists, will also open doors for mission work. Both curative and preventative care can benefit the communities lacking such personnel. The relationships that develop between the healthcare providers and the patients can provide opportunities to share the gospel. Medical training can be provided to local Christians to make patient care and witness more culturally appropriate. Such ministries may be especially appropriate for missionaries from Asia; it is likely that the ethnicity of the medical provider, even when a foreigner, will influence the doors that will open. A bi-vocational missionary observed that Asian-American physicians are better received by people in the Middle East population than European-American physicians (personal communication, January 4, 2009).

Financial services, such as microloans and financial training, can be provided according to local needs, in compliance with local regulations. If the beneficiaries create successful businesses, they can repay their loans, creating a sustainable model that can also benefit relatives and friends, and creating opportunities to share the gospel accordingly.

Employees of state-owned enterprises can be bi-vocational missionaries to creative access nations. Project managers, engineers, legal service providers, computer system analysts, graphic designers, teachers, and researchers in academia can use their skills to secure long-term professional visas in these 10/40 window countries (Wei *et al.*, 2016). Transportation workers such as railway workers, truck drivers, automobile mechanics, gas station managers, and longshore and harbor workers are all potential missionaries. These professionals can reach out to customers or local co-workers for small scale bible study opportunities.

Cultural exchange programs that involve teachers of English

and Chinese, as well as language students can provide opportunities to live in and serve in creative access nations for relatively short periods, typically one to two years. Nevertheless, a prolonged stay with any limited-term visa is likely to be considered unethical and will arouse suspicions from the local immigration officers.

Trade and manufacturing are also good platforms for outreach. Crafts or clothing made locally can be sold via eBay or other web-based merchandise platforms. A plan was proposed by expatriates in China a decade ago to set up Christian-based contact points every one hundred miles along the land-based Silk Road Economic Belt (A tentmaking missionary in China, personal communication, 18th September 2011). These contact points can provide goods and services as diverse as fuel stations, restaurants, hotels, factories for manufactured goods, companies for the energy industry, cell phones, small commodities, restaurant supplies, and real estate consumables. These businesses enhance the local economy by providing employment and revenue for the local government. They also provide opportunities for Christians to network, both for support and encouragement and for outreach and evangelism.

Housemaids (especially those from the Philippines) are serving in homes in the Middle East and other locations typically closed to professional missionaries. Their interaction with the younger generations may sow gospel seeds to be harvested in the future.

Social services can be provided through Non-Government Organizations (NGOs). These services include, but are not limited to, poverty reduction and disaster relief. Even retirees may move to a community and serve in or fund a local nonprofit organization. Especially important services offered by NGOs in developing nations focus on wells and clean water delivery systems, providing not only the needed water but also opportunities to share the gospel in the local context. Clean water not only improves local sanitation but also expands the local arable land. Further economic development is possible through the installation of greenhouses and the introduction of vertical and organic farming. Women's shelters can be established in contexts where the need exists. The opportunities for teachers, consultants, and counselors are virtually limitless in developing countries.

For those more interested in social justice, anti-trafficking NGOs in Southeast Asia and India are needed (George, 2013; Shellnutt, 2017). Christians can cooperate with law enforcement and existing NGOs, providing services and education to the victims to help them reintegrate into society.

All outreach to the indigenous people along the BRI route should be holistic, given the great needs that exist among them. Community development and evangelism should occur simultaneously. The platforms above merely provide an entry point. Sharing the gospel and a church planting strategy that is reproducible by the national church should be emphasized from the beginning. Any local believers should be included in the initial planning and should take significant responsibilities from the beginning, with the goal of transferring all leadership responsibilities to them when possible. The initial outreach strategy may focus on a top-down approach (targeting the leaders of the local community first), a bottom-up approach (targeting the grassroots population first), or both simultaneously. Mission organizations and seminaries need to equip future missionaries with the necessary skills.

Mission Challenges Associated with the BRI

The BRI is still in the early days of its development. The Asian Infrastructure Investment Bank has been formed, and several projects have been approved and construction has begun (AIIB, 2018). However, significant challenges remain at several levels, including political, economic, technological, and spiritual, all of which affect those attempting to bring the Gospel to the unreached.

Political Challenges

The ability of missionaries to stay in a country depends on the country's policies and international relations, especially if there is a risk of war. The building of artificial islands, airports, and military facilities in the South China Sea by China has been viewed as a military threat by the USA and several countries in South East Asia (Phillips, 2018). A small mishap could lead to a full-fledged war. All activities, missionary and non-missionary, along the maritime route would inevitably be disrupted if a war occurs.

The decision to join or reject the BRI also elicits serious debate within the countries potentially affected. For example, the second-largest state of Australia, Victoria, has decided to join the BRI despite opposition from the national government in Canberra (Australian Broadcasting Corporation, 2018). Similar disagreements among government entities have occurred in Kazakhstan, Malaysia, and even England. Such internal division may potentially lead to political instability, especially in developing countries. The bilateral relationships that China has formed with various countries may be more fluid than solid. Whether a country honors an agreement depends on who is in power. A change in government may result in the annulation of an agreement. These factors may make it difficult to maintain a constant missionary presence and witness.

Economic and Technological Challenges
The development of technology has resulted in various interregional and transnational criminal organizations developing the potential to disrupt the functioning of any organization. Organized crime frequently focuses on cybercrimes and the trafficking of people, drugs, antiquities, and wildlife. Organized crime is especially prevalent in Russia, Kazakhstan, Lithuania, the Czech Republic, Poland, and Bangladesh. (Lo, *et al.*, 2020) The presence of such criminality may significantly slow the development of a country's economy.

Corruption in developing countries is among the greatest challenges the BRI faces (Balding, 2018a). Opaque transactions between the leaders of the nations involved and the Chinese government are common, especially concerning procurement and the quality control of construction. What constitutes bribery varies by culture. Central Asia government officials may believe it is completely appropriate to ask for a cash gift to approve a license application. Some law enforcement officers require a "protection fee or security fee" from business owners who risk being shut down if they do not pay (A tentmaking missionary in Kazakhstan, personal communication, 28th September 2018). However, Christians may not believe that such transactions are ethical.

Refusal to pay bribes may close the door to missionary visas, building permits, or the right to assemble. To combat bribery and corruption and to have a successful ministry in such contexts, Christians need to pray for wisdom, good relationships with government officials, and cultural transformation (Fung, 2010).

The USA-China tariff war is a manifestation of each country's desire for world dominance economically and politically (Warsh, 2018; Shan, 2019) The U.S. sanctions limiting technology exportation to China is affecting China's economy (Thomson, 2015). The USA has also made other threats to China, including revoking China's status as a developing country in the World Trade Organization (Amaro, 2018) and imposing restrictions on the US-Mexico-Canada trade agreement so that parts made in China will have higher tariffs even if they come through Mexico or Canada (Balding, 2018b). Another minor threat is to revoke the international postal service agreement so that China will have to pay more to mail packages to the USA (Lardieri, 2018). Both countries want to have greater influence upon the actions of the other, and over other countries.

Some Asian countries have realized that they might be getting caught in a financial trap as the BRI infrastructure becomes operational (Ching, 2018). One example is the container terminal port in Sri Lanka. The country received a loan from China for its construction. However, the revenue from the port has been much lower than expected and the country was not able to pay back the loan on schedule. Therefore, Sri Lanka renegotiated the loan, giving the Chinese 70% equity in the port and a 99-year lease, essentially putting the port under the control of the Chinese government semi-permanently.

Chinese state-owned enterprises sign agreements with developing countries to build infrastructure and develop their economies that often stipulate that construction will be done by Chinese companies. This means that few local nationals are employed in these projects (Hai & Cohen, 2017). These companies hire primarily Chinese workers, including Chinese farmers brought to the country to grow Chinese vegetables and produce Chinese food for the new Chinese community (A tentmaking missionary in

Kazakhstan, personal communication, October 3, 2008). Relations between local nationals and the Chinese deteriorate rapidly under such conditions.

The different railway standards among the countries have created greater technological challenges than foreseen for non-stop train service from China to Europe. Different countries have different gauge standards (Hillman, 2018; Hodgkinson, 2016). This mismatched track width inevitably creates delays. For example, the first freight train from China to England covered 7,780 miles in eighteen days, approximately 450 miles per day. If the train traveled for only 8 hours each day, the average speed was merely 56 miles per hour, slower than transportation by truck, and far from the high-speed train target of 200 miles per hour. Standardizing gauge size among the countries or advanced flexible and safe train axles has continued to present challenges.

In contrast to the German proposal of Industry 4.0 focusing on the automation of manufacturing and industrial practices (Manske-Wang, 2020), China has proposed the goal of "Made in China 2025," moving China's focus in manufacturing from cheap, low-tech products to 11 high-tech fields where China can become a leading manufacturer (Holslag, 2019). Such goals are based on the assumption that the country's economy continues to grow, but this is not guaranteed.

Because the social and political stability of the region depends so heavily on technological and economic development, these challenges may limit the development of the BRI and missionary opportunities.

Spiritual Challenges
The evangelization of the very religiously and culturally diverse peoples associated with the BRI will require numerous, focused strategies. The 10/40 Window is 9000 miles wide and home to a variety of Muslims, Hindus, Buddhists, Atheists, and Animists. As the population becomes more mobile due to the BRI, mixed marriages will become more frequent and the future generations will have less clear religious identities. The children of a Buddhist father and a Hindu mother will likely be influenced by both

religions. With four billion non-Christians in this region, there is an urgent need for equipping a large number of professional missionaries for effective evangelism, discipleship training, and church planting in these new and developing contexts.

Beyond the need to reach the unreached, there is also an urgent need for a concerted effort from Chinese churches and non-Chinese organizations to help the persecuted Christians in China. The Chinese Communist Party passed a law in February 2018 that put the house churches under extreme scrutiny, requiring registration with the local government offices (World Watch Monitor, 2018). This ordinance has been regularly enforced since June 2018. Sales of the Bible through online stores and non-church bookstores have been forbidden (Johnson, 2018; Sandeman, 2018) and children under eighteen have been prohibited from attending these churches. Millions of surveillance cameras are installed in different cities throughout the country. They are used to identify church leaders and those associated with them. Thousands of Chinese house church leaders are either under persecution, have been forced to leave the country, or are prohibited from returning to the country under the new policy (Cheng, 2019). The working visas of many Western missionaries have been terminated (Yan, 2018; Yu, 2017). This has created a leadership vacuum. There are few who have the necessary experience and are able to coordinate missionary work within China, such as linking exiled Chinese Christian leaders with Western organizations and providing missionary training to those in the underground house churches. Nevertheless, Chinese churches have envisioned sending twenty thousand missionaries from their own communities to evangelize the least reached by 2030 (Zylstra, 2016). This number of Chinese missionaries can only be mobilized if there is better coordination from outside the country as indigenous sending organizations are illegal within the country. This coordination should be done not just by the Chinese outside of China but should include Western organizations to benefit from their expertise.

Moreover, the quality of theological training provided to potential missionaries by Chinese churches is not comparable to the training available in Western countries (Breimert, 1999; Ruokanen,

1999). Typical missionary training schools admit students with only a high school diploma and a passion for missions. Training typically includes a two-year internship and teaching in a local church. These graduates are then sent as missionaries to rural areas of China or to foreign countries, often in Southeast Asia and Central Asia. Seminaries which offer bachelors-level and graduate-level training are limited in China. Although many Chinese Christians go overseas for seminary training, those who return to China are too few to respond to the need. The limitations of existing training will make meeting the goal of sending twenty thousand missionaries by 2030 difficult. However, if high-quality online training programs or other creative educational approaches from the West can be developed, reaching the goal may still be possible.

Outlook and Conclusions

Ephesians 5:16 and Colossians 4:5 speak of "making the most of the opportunity," emphasizing the importance of making good use of every door that opens. There are four billion non-Christians with various worldviews, cultures, and religions within the 10/40 Window. We need wisdom concerning how to share the gospel with them strategically. However, good strategies are not enough; planting churches also requires the Holy Spirit's guidance and protection. We need to be as shrewd as snakes and as innocent as doves (Matt. 10:16).

We do not know to what degree the BRI will come to fruition and to what extent it will link the world to China. Similarly, we do not know how long the open door that now allows Christians to enter countries such as Tajikistan, Uzbekistan, and Turkmenistan will remain open. After the fall of the Soviet Union, the doors closed in less than ten years, as Muslims rose in rank in these countries' administration (Kim, 2014; Mounstephen, 2019). Factories in China are now moving out of the country because of economic factors associated with the tariff and trade war. No one can foresee the changes that will occur due to the evolution of economic forces and international relations in Eurasia. The equipping of Chinese missionaries cannot be sustained if the economy or international relations deteriorate. Therefore, we need to make good use of the current openness of these countries. The flow of Christians and Christian materials should be promoted to evangelize pre-believers, equip disciples, and plant indigenous churches. Once a country's government believes that openness to outsiders is no longer a good policy, the window of opportunity for evangelization will be closed, and the persecution of Christians may even follow.

The current leaders of the Communist Party in China have created hurdles which hinder the spread of the gospel, but which have also alienated the population. After COVID-19, there is increased opposition within China to the ruling party (Wang & Hernández, 2020). Perhaps this opposition, combined with forces from outside the country, may motivate the Chinese Communist Party to reform its policies due to disillusionment with Communist ideology and the desire for greater human rights. If China were to embrace human rights, the surveillance, control, and persecution of Chinese Christians would come to an end. This would enable Chinese churches to train thousands of missionaries, either via external help or with the help of returning Chinese expatriates, enabling the fulfillment of the vision of sending out twenty thousand missionaries by the year 2030 (Zylstra, 2016). If China becomes a missionary-sending country, and the infrastructure of the BRI permits the exchange of people, goods, and ideas throughout Eurasia, perhaps, the gospel can be preached to all the nations sooner than foreseen.

References

AIIB. (2018). Asian Infrastructure Investment Bank Annual Report. Retrieved from https://www.aiib.org/en/news-events/annual-report/2018/home/index.html

AIIB. (2020). Asian Infrastructure Investment Bank Fact Sheet. Retrieved from https://www.aiib.org/en/treasury/ common/ download/AIIB FACT-SHEET 05282020.pdf

AIIB Agreements. (2015). Headquarters Agreement between the Government of the People's Republic of China and the Asian Infrastructure Investment Bank. Retrieved from https://www.aiib.org/en/about-aiib/basic-documents/ download/headquarters-agreement/headquarters-agreement.pdf

AIIB Partnership. (2019). Partnerships with Asian Infrastructure Investment Bank. Retrieved from https://www.aiib.org/en/about-aiib/who-we-are/partnership/index.html

Amaro, S. (2018). Trump is trying to 'de-globalize' the Chinese and US economies, former WTO chief says. Retrieved from https://www.cnbc.com/2018/10/08/trump-is-trying-to-de-globalize-the-chinese-and-us-economies-former-wto-chief-says.html

Australian Broadcasting Corporation. (2018). One belt, one road: Victoria signs MOU to join China's controversial global trade initiative. Retrieved from https://www.abc.net.au/news/2018-10-26/victoria-and-china-belt-and-road-signing-mou/10435148

Balding, C. (2018a). How the U.S.-Mexico pact could turn tables on China. Retrieved from https://www.bloomberg.com/opinion/articles/2018-08-29/u-s-mexico-pact-could-turn-the-tables-on-china

Balding, C. (2018b). Why democracies are turning against belt and road. *Foreign Affairs*. Retrieved from https://www.foreignaffairs.com/articles/china/2018-10-24/why-democracies-are-turning-against-belt-and-road

Breimert, D. (1999). Theological Education in China: A Survey on the Contemporary Situation in Mainland China and Hong Kong. *Svensk missionstidskrift, 87*(4), 517-553.

Browne, A. (2016). Cast in Concrete: China's Problem With Excess. *The Wall Street Journal*. Retrieved from https://www.wsj.com/articles/cast-in-concrete-chinas-problem-with-excess-1461038709

Center for Strategic and International Studies (2017). How Much Trade Transits the South China Sea? Retrieved from https://chinapower.csis.org/much-trade-transits-south-china-sea/

Cheng, J. (2019). Expelled from China. *World Magazine*. Retrieved from https://world.wng.org/2019/01/expelled_from_china

Ching, F. (2018). China 'belt and road' could be a debt trap. *The Japan Times*. Retrieved from https://www.japantimes.co.jp/opinion/2018/08/28/commentary/world-commentary/chinas-belt-road-debt-trap/#.XsSRAmhKg2x

Farr, T. F. D. (2019). Diplomacy and Persecution in China. *First Things, 293*, 29. Retrieved from http://www.firstthings.com/ (Publisher's URL:)

Fung, J. M. (2010). A Corruption-Ridden World: Think Global, Respond Local, as a Filipino Church. *Landas, 24*(1), 85-104.

George, A. (2013). Finding Hope in a Broken World: The Response of the Church to Human Trafficking. *Landas, 27*(1), 103-109.

Hai, H., and Cohen, A. (2017). China is Africa's biggest economic partner, but what role for the United States? Retrieved from https://www.forbes.com/sites/realspin/2017/10/18/china-is-africas-biggest-economic-partner-but-what-role-for-the-united-states/#6bda19637f43

Hillman, J. E. (2018). The Rise of China-Europe Railways. Retrieved from https://www.csis.org/analysis/rise-china-europe-railways#

Hodgkinson, P. J. (2016). Development of seamless rail-based intermodal transport services in Northeast and Central Asia. Retrieved from https://www.unescap.org/sites/default/files/Seamless%20Transport%2 oreport_Kazakhstan.pdf

Holslag, J. (2019). *The Silk Road Trap*. Cambridge, England: Polity Press.

Johnson, I. (2018). China Bans Online Bible Sales as It Tightens Religious Controls. Retrieved from https://www.nytimes.com/2018/04/05/world/asia/china-bans-bible-sales.html

Kaarieni, Y. M., and Tuah, S. N. (2019). Analysis of Ecotourism Development Strategy in Tanjung Puting Province National Park, Central Kalimantan. *KnE Social Sciences, 2020*, 966-978.

Kim, D. (2014). 25 Years of Central Asia Mission – Part 2. Retrieved from https://www.intercp.org/2014/06/25-years-of-central-asia-mission-part-2/

Lardieri, A. (2018). U.S. to withdraw from international postal agreement. Retrieved from https://www.usnews.com/news/politics/articles/2018-10-17/us-to-withdraw-from-international-postal-agreement

Lim, T. W., Chan, H., Tseng K., and Lim, W.X. (2016). *China's One Belt One Road Initiative*. London: Imperial College Press.

Lo, T. W., Siegel, D., and Kwok, S. I. (2020). *Organized crime and corruption across borders: exploring the Belt and Road Initiative*. Milton Park, Abingdon, Oxon ; New York, NY: Routledge.

Lu, D. (2019). Everyday Modernity in China: From Danwei to the "World Factory.". *Fudan Journal of the Humanities & Social Sciences, 12*(1), 79.

Manske-Wang, W. (2020). *Opportunities and challenges of BRI for German SMEs: Analyses and recommendations based on a cross-cultural view*. In H. Pechlaner, Erschbamer, Greta, Thees, Hannes, and Gruber, Mirjam (Ed.), *China and the New Silk Road Challenges and Impacts on the regional and local level*.

Marsh, J. (2014). Afro-Chinese marriages boom in Guangzhou: but will it be 'til death do us part"? *Post Magazine*. Retrieved from https://www.scmp.com/magazines/post-magazine/article/1521076/afro-chinese-marriages-boom-guangzhou-will-it-be-til-death

McCarthy, N. (2018). China Produces More Cement Than The Rest Of The World Combined Retrieved from https://www.forbes.com/sites/niallmccarthy/2018/07/06/china-produces-more-cement-than-the-rest-of-the-world-combined-infographic/#2ae2524a6881

Ministry of Foreign Affairs. (2013). President Xi Jinping Delivers Important Speech and Proposes to Build a Silk Road Economic Belt with Central Asian Countries. Retrieved from https://www.fmprc.gov.cn/mfa_eng/topics_665678/xjpfwzysiesgjtfhsh zzfh_665686/t1076334.shtml

Mounstephen, P. (2019). Bishop of Truro's Independent Review for the Foreign Secretary of FCO Support for Persecuted Christians Interim Report. Retrieved from https://christianpersecutionreview.org.uk/interim-report/

Nunno, R. (2018). Fact Sheet: High Speed Rail Development Worldwide. Retrieved from https://www.eesi.org/papers/view/fact-sheet-high-speed-rail-development-worldwide

Nunoo, F. E. (2014). China's security challenge in Africa. Retrieved from http://africachinareporting.co.za/2014/07/chinas-security-challenge-in-africa/

Park, J. S.-H. (2015). Chosen to fulfill the Great Commission?: Biblical and theological reflections on the Back to Jerusalem: vision of Chinese churches. *Missiology, 43*(AD 2000), 163-174.

Phillips, T. (2018). Photos show Beijing's militarisation of South China Sea in new detail. *The Guardian*. Retrieved from https://www.theguardian.com/world/2018/feb/06/photos-beijings-militarisation-south-china-sea-philippines

Purdy, M. (2013). China's economy, in six charts. *Harvard Business Review*. Retrieved from https://hbr.org/2013/11/chinas-economy-in-six-charts

Ruokanen, M. (1999). Theological Education in China: A Summary of Three NIME Presentations and Other Discussions. *Svensk missionstidskrift, 87*(4), 491-508. Retrieved from http://www.teol.uu.se/ (Publisher's URL:)

Sandeman, J. (2018). You Can Still Buy a Bible in China Retrieved from https://www.eternitynews.com.au/world/you-can-still-buy-a-bible-in-china/

Shan, W. (2019). The Unwinnable Trade War: Everyone Loses in the U.S.-Chinese Clash-but Especially Americans. *Foreign Affairs, 98*(6), 99-108.

Shellnutt, K. (2017). Bringing Light to the Trafficking Fight: How Christians' Broad-based Strategies are Making Big Progress in Cambodia. *Christianity Today, 61*(5), 26-32.

Stafford, T., and Hattaway, P. (2004). A captivating vision: why Chinese house churches may just end up fulfilling the Great Commission. *Christianity Today, 48*(4), 84-86.

Thomson, I. (2015). US govt bans intel from selling chips to China's supercomputer boffins. Retrieved from https://www.theregister.co.uk/2015/04/10/us_intel_china_ban/

Wang, B. (2014). Partnerships. Retrieved from https://www.aiib.org/en/about-aiib/who-we-are/partnership/index.html

Wang, V., and Hernández, J. C. . (2020). Coronavirus Crisis Awakens a Sleeping Giant: China's Youth. Retrieved from https://www.nytimes.com/2020/03/28/world/asia/coronavirus-china-youth.html

Warsh, K. (2018). A U.S.-China trade war would cause "shock for the global economy". Retrieved from https://www.thestreet.com/video/kevin-warsh-a-u-s-china-trade-war-would-cause-shock-for-the-global-economy-14764854147648544

Wei, Y., Zhang, Z., and Zhu, B. (2016). *Zhong Ying "yi dai yi lu" zhan lüe he zuo yan jiu = Research on Sino-British strategic cooperation under framework of the Belt and Road initiative* (Di 1 ban. ed.). Beijing Shi: She hui ke xue wen xian chu ban she.

World Watch Monitor. (2018). China's new religion regulations expected to increase pressure on Christians. Retrieved from https://www.worldwatchmonitor.org/2018/02/chinas-new-religion-regulations-expected-increase-pressure-christians/

Yan, A. (2018). Overseas NGOs in China uneasy about new oversight law. Retrieved from https://www.scmp.com/news/china/policies-politics/article/2039279/overseas-ngos-china-uneasy-about-new-oversight-law

Yu, V. (2017). Draft Chinese law puts NGOs' future on the line. Retrieved from https://www.scmp.com/news/china/policies-politics/article/1816097/draft-chinese-law-puts-ngos-future-line

Zhang, S., and Su, J. (2019). China's iron and steel association warns on over-capacity, shrinking profits. Retrieved from https://www.reuters.com/article/us-china-steel/chinas-iron-and-steel-association-warns-on-over-capacity-shrinking-profits-idUSKCN1S404D

Zylstra, S. E. (2016). Made in China: The Next Mass Missionary Movement: Chinese Christians plan to send 20,000 missionaries by 2030. *Christianity Today, 60*(1), 20-21. Retrieved from http://www.christianitytoday.com/ct/archives/

About the Author

Paul Lee (pseudonym) is a graduate of the Master of Arts in Missiology program, Southwestern Baptist Theological Seminary. He is involved in equipping and mobilizing churches for missions. He has served as a bi-vocational missionary overseas for five years. He can be reached at Paullee2100@yahoo.com.

GREAT COMMISSION
RESEARCH JOURNAL
2021, Vol. 13(1) 39-60

How Research on Young Adults Informs Evangelism

Gary Comer

Abstract

In a time when the church is missing members of the younger generations, it is important to look to generational research and listen to compelling voices regarding currents in the culture, with the aim of informing evangelism among these generations. This treatise provides an analysis of two missiological-relevant aspects of these generations: profile and receptivity. Based on this analysis, the author proposes correctives to increase the effectiveness of evangelistic efforts.

Introduction

Scanning the roughly 200-person church service, making a mental note of the many older adults in the chairs, my visceral reaction was, "Where are all the young people?" Though the scene was marred, like a masterpiece painting with missing brushstrokes, what I observed that January, 2019, morning at a campus of The Summit Church in North Carolina (pastored by SBC President J. D. Greear) was no surprise. Based on the data available (Barna Group, 2020; Clydesdale and Garces-Foley, 2019), this church is not an outlier. The demographics of this church were not a surprise for me, nor would they be for anyone who has observed what has been reported across the ecclesial spectrum. Even prominent churches such as this one does not know how to reach and retain the younger generations.

Having a noticeable demographic missing from church is a problem. When the next generations are missing, the church's growth and future are threatened. Thus, when the Great Commission Research Network chose to address this topic at its conference in 2019, I saw a worthy research project to pursue. This article allows me to put into writing the key concepts which surfaced from that study, to not only document my findings, but also to contribute to solving this puzzle challenging the 21st century church.

For those of us from among the older generations, relating to and reaching members of the younger generations can seem intimidating, if not impossible. When I joined a very young staff at Sandals Church when I was in my late forties, people glared at my gas-guzzling SUV and my belted phone holder. They kept asking, "How old are you?" Although I may not have been as generationally attuned as I should have been, serving for five years at that youthful megachurch opened my mind to alternative ways of thinking, especially concerning evangelism.

This overview of generational research focuses on developing applications to reach younger generations with the gospel, not on merely reporting generational characteristics. Amid my analysis, I have threaded practical insights to inform evangelism. This will lead to the rationale for why I favor a particular biblical approach, along with three guiding directives aimed at improving our efforts. First, we must begin with what we know of these younger generations.

The Young Adult Vacuum in Churches

The need for the church to attract and integrate younger members is urgent. The Barna Group's (2020) pre-pandemic article *The State of the Church: What's on the Minds of America's Pastors*, reported that half of the study's participants listed their top concerns as (1) declining evangelism by members and (2) reaching a younger audience. With layers of complexity, this issue is a conundrum, a puzzling but not-yet-solved mystery.

And if one enigma were not enough, we now have 2020's COVID-19 pandemic, racial-injustice unrest, and the increasing political and cultural polarization to consider in understanding today's generations. But from God's perspective, these phenomena are not occurring haphazardly. They will be used to serve his purposes, as will be the leaders of his people whom he has chosen. As Paul described how he was "set apart" from his mother's womb (Gal 1:15), Jesus has chosen leaders to serve his church in such times. May the ideas presented here equip such leaders to meet the challenge!

The Square Peg Soul

Many of us have a way of thinking about generational outreach implanted in our collective memory. Some of us remember the revolutionary attractional model of church, the seeker-focused Willow Creek model originated by Bill Hybels of Willow Creek (1975), and further developed by Rick Warren (1980). Saddleback Church was first to profile their target audience whom they called "Saddleback Sam." He represented a typical person who was living in Saddleback Valley suburbs. His characteristics and needs helped define how the church would strategically reach its community. In 1993, Willow Creek followed with their own profile of an unchurched target audience, described in the book *Inside the Mind of Unchurched Harry and Mary*, assuming again that the description would help the church effectively reach the people in its community (Strobel, 2007).

Following this logic, should we not simply define "Millennial Matthew" or "Gen Z Zoe" and provide programs which attract them to the church? If it is safe to conclude that our younger constituents have common characteristics, why have we not defined who they are in order to develop the corresponding programs and tools to draw them to Christ and his church? This is a key question. However, a simple, typical profile of today's young adults may not be possible, pulling us into a dilemma.

To understand why a typical profile may not exist, we need to objectively examine the data collected on this generation. In my quest for the best resources, Oxford University Press's *The Twenty-*

something Soul: Understanding the Religious and Secular Lives of Young Adults by Tim Clydesdale and Kathleen Garces-Foley (2019), became my preferred source of information. It is a broad, academic study that is reasonably objective. Since twenty-somethings include younger Millennials and older members of Gen Z, I will use the following terms interchangeably, "those born in the 90s," "young adults," and "twenty-somethings." Although referenced at times, I am not including younger members of Gen Z or the younger members of the generation Jean Twenge (2017) calls iGen or the iPhone generation (those who are currently teenagers).

Clydesdale and Garces-Foley's (2019) findings are based on the 2013 National Study of American Twentysomethings (NSAT) which includes longitudinal data from 1,818 survey participants collected over several years and numerous in-depth interviews of young adults in their twenties. The research found that young adulthood is a period of development where behaviors and values are quite fluid (Clydesdale & Garces-Foley, 2019, p. 149–51). This observation provides both a warning and hope concerning our current situation: Twenty-something believers can lose faith, while spiritually-distanced twenty-somethings can acquire it. The interviews affirmed the plasticity of their beliefs, often linked to notable life events such as changes in community, friends, location, school, and partner, marital, and parenthood status. Their beliefs today are not fixed, and we should never take the faith of those who are believers for granted or consider non-believers as without potential for faith.

Analysis: Generational Profiles

To answer why we do not have a Millennial Matthew or Gen Z Zoe, we can look at Clydesdale and Garces-Foley's conclusion. They describe twenty-somethings as "America's most truly pluralist generation of adults" (Clydesdale & Garces-Foley, 2019, p. 184). The most dominant characteristic of twenty-somethings is that they have few, if any, characteristics in common. As CNN pundit Van Jones has noted of younger voters, it is "the most diverse generation ever." (Jones, 2020). More than preceding generations, they are pluralistic in beliefs, views, and backgrounds. So, a graphic such as

Saddleback Sam cannot exist. It is not possible to describe a typical person in their twenties today.

Although some important generalizations can be made about this generation, the research does not support a simple profile concerning their values, their beliefs, and what might help them to progress spiritually. If we were to seek to profile today's twenty-somethings, as was done for the white Boomers of Southern California's 1980 suburbia (i.e., Saddleback Sam), we might need 7 or 8 different profiles to describe the same proportion of the population that was described by Saddleback's single profile.

What would it look like if we tried to create a single profile for Millennial Matthew or Gen Z Zoe? Although the characteristics observed to create a description of yesterday's boomers and the characteristics observed to create a description of today's twenty-somethings are quite different, the domains of observations are similar. Concerning their religious identity, in addition to evangelical, four other major identities exist. The twenty-somethings in Clydesdale and Garces-Foley's (2019) study identified as following:

30% Evangelical
18% Roman Catholic
14% Mainline Protestant
9% Other Religions
29% No religious identity

Additionally, the research revealed four categories of "Nones" (those with no religious identity). Most were *Indifferent Secularists* (54%), young adults who do not prioritize pursuing meaning in their life. In contrast the *Philosophic Secularists* (12%) pursue a philosophic view of life's ultimate meaning yet reject religious faith; this would include many atheists. A third group, *Spiritual Eclectics* (17%), includes those who embrace a spiritual view of life coming from a mixture of influences. Fourthly are *Unaffiliated Believers* (17%) who believe in God but who are either "Dones," those having given up on the church, or those who have distanced themselves from church involvement and association for at least the moment

(Clydesdale & Garces-Foley, 2018, p. 155).

Compounding the diversity even further, we could similarly divide the 9% who identified with "Other Religions" into Muslims, Jews, Mormons, Buddhists, Sikhs, Hindus, and others. My Imam friend fits within this category, along with the hundreds of all ages who attend our neighborhood's mosque daily. This category, which represents a very broad range of religions, is sure to grow as America continues to become more diverse.

How Research Informs Evangelism: Pluralistic Range

It is important to note that young non-religious adults have widely divergent beliefs. *Thus, evangelism to younger generations cannot be based on one single approach or one specific form of presenting the gospel; but rather the approach to evangelization should be determined by the non-believer's spiritual stance; we should bring them from their particular point of departure to the knowledge of Christ. In short, we need a dynamic evangelistic approach that adapts to the needs and experiences of each twenty-something with whom we want to share the gospel. We must have the discernment necessary to share with them in a resonant and effectual fashion.*

Because so many young adults today are far from believing in Christ, evangelism must be built around giving them the opportunity for processing the message and its implications. James Emory White, in *Meet Generation Z* (2017), mirrors that conclusion in the chapter Rethinking Evangelism, "The most foundational rethinking is one that in previous writings and in multiple settings I've sketched out to try to persuade pastors and church leaders of one foundational dynamic: the importance of process" (p. 107). It was from seeing ineffective evangelistic "presentation" models that led me to design an evangelism approach called the *Relational Evangelism Process* (Comer, 2013) and to define an assortment of practical faith-sharing skills.

Here are some "process" skills I believe all believers need to have in their repertoire:

Framing: The skill of inviting someone into an ongoing conversation. It can be used when building a relationship, learning together, or discussing a question or objection.

Safety: The skill of reducing risk in a relationship enough to enable open, honest conversations. This is where we communicate that whoever the person is, and whatever the person believes or expresses, will not alter the friendship.

Drawing: The skill of asking deeper questions in order to draw out a person's true thoughts and feelings. This practice affords vital information to deepen the dialogue and get to the place of spiritual influence (Comer, 2018, p. 332).

These skills are similar to those due to the Holy Spirit's influence on Philip in Acts 8, directing him to "get beside the eunuch," and then "stay there" for a time, and finally to step up into the chariot to share in a conversational journey (See Acts 8:29–31). These are "positioning" skills. Every spiritually related expression of interest, question, or objection can be leveraged into an exploratory dialogue.

In essence, in our attempt to reach this demographic, we need to broaden our evangelistic focus from merely proclaiming the gospel to discerning what it takes to have "influence" on a twenty-something, motivating them to be receptive to, and enabling the necessary processing of, the gospel message. This change of emphasis from proclamation to influence is essential but difficult. Given their diversity of beliefs, how will we know what they understand of the gospel?

Analysis: Gospel Receptivity

Many of us are familiar with common generational categories (Table 1). For analyzing how the gospel might be disseminated, a basic question is to ask if generational distinctions influence how the gospel is received. If we are to better understand how to reach younger generations, we must answer the question: *Is the generational shift of such a nature that it alters how people are influenced?* Does it affect the way a person receives, hears, and responds to the gospel?

Generation	Approximate Birth Years	Influential World Events and Phenomena
Baby Boomers	1946-1964	JFK's assassination (Early Boomers), Watergate, Energy Crisis, Cold War
Gen X	1965-1980	Challenger, Berlin Wall, Gulf War, Rodney King
Millennials	1981-1995	Columbine, 9/11, War in Iraq
Gen Z	1996-2012	iPhones, texting, terrorism, school shootings, gender diversity, COVID-19

Table 1. *Common Generational Categories*

In my book, *Soul Whisperer,* I argued that such a shift did indeed take place between the Baby Boomers and Generation X (Comer, 2013, p. 30–41). I built a case that the modern-to-postmodern transition was a change in culture that influenced gospel receptivity. Here, I am referring to "postmodern" as a broad cultural outlook, not the philosophy that cast doubts upon the certainties created by modernism. It is rather the realism that followed a period of idealism, similar to Disney's vision of Tomorrow Land being followed by the MA-rated programs of today's Netflix. During the transition, pop culture evolved when the Boomer-led hair metal bands of the 80s were unseated by the darker-emotive angst of Gen X-led grunge bands, with Nirvana's *Smells Like Teen Spirit* (1991) leading the way in reshaping the rock world (cf. Loudwire, 2021, "How Grunge Killed Hair Metal").

Postmodernism's emergence, which some have dated by the fall of the Berlin Wall in 1989, led to the death of an assumption within the church (Oden, 1995). Suddenly, effectively communicating the gospel focused, not on perfectionism, moralism, or scientific and economic progress, but on present experiences, relationships, and un-pretentious honesty. Focusing on how people are, not how they should be, became the center of all parts of society including language and church.

Understanding this historic change is a prerequisite to evaluating the experience of twenty-somethings. The question we must ask about those born in the 1990s and early 2000s, is whether a generational shift has altered how people are influenced by the gospel. My readings and personal observations lead me to conclude that such a shift has not occurred. Let me qualify and explain what I mean. Understanding generational changes for the sake of effectively communicating the gospel seems prudent at face value. But do these changes, such as increased use of computer-mediated communication, change how people hear and understand the gospel?

If those born in the 90s received meaningful life-changing information from nothing but their electronic devices, this would be a major shift in human nature. The church would have to radically change how it communicated the gospel. Although a high percentage of the younger generations are proficient in computer-mediated communication, online addictions and isolation are growing problems (Clydesdale & Garces Foley, 2019, p. 158). Because of these problems, the presumption that social media is the main force influencing their faith is not defensible. This does not mean that young adults do not consume online information, nor that they are immune to what they see and hear on media. Rather, important aspects of life, such as developing one's faith or making major decisions, are not primarily influenced by social media or church advertising, which are more similar to background noise than the primary forces which influence them. Rarely will people say that they have been influenced by social media or church advertising. This is no different than previous generations.

Alan Noble agues in *Disruptive Witness* (2018) that we should not focus on improving media communication with young people, but rather on capturing their attention and meaningfully engaging them. Noble's thesis is that our addiction to electronic devices has left us so wearied and distracted that we fail to process information, especially the gospel, beyond the surface level. "The modern mind is often not prepared to engage in dialogue about personally challenging ideas, particularly ones with deep implications. The fatigued mind would rather categorize a conversation about God as another superficial distraction" (Noble, 2018, p. 21). Thus, he argues that we need to provide a "disruptive witness."

Jean Twenge, in her book *iGen* (2017), argues those born after 1994 need "in person" relationships to be healthier and happier (Twenge, 299). Moreover, in order to rectify the consequences of distraction and shallowness, we need real, incarnate relationships as the seedbed for deeper searching and dialogue (Frost, 2014, p. 11–12). This need for meaningful connections has been exacerbated by the coronavirus pandemic which has increased the desire for meeting with others. Although non-believers may be less welcoming of sharing a physical space with strangers, they may be more welcoming of those with whom they are familiar and whom they trust. In fact, in this new world, establishing a relationship is now a prerequisite for communicating with others. Such personal connection can occur through a phone, Zoom, or messaging.

How Research Informs Evangelism: Meaningful Communication

The Missional Behavior Survey, a study conducted by Christ Together, revealed that 73 percent of Christians saw themselves as ineffective in sharing the gospel with nonbelievers (Kozey, 2014). Most church members see themselves as lacking knowledge, confidence, and the ability to influence others. The research indicates that "authentic-meaningful conversation" is valued more by younger generations than by older generations. A popular television series for the younger generations is *The 100*, based on the book by the millennial Kass Morgan, which focuses on moral dilemmas. Through seven seasons, the characters never stop having deep, gut-wrenching conversations about who they are, what they did, and what they should do. Comparing this type of conversation to the message that churches communicate to those who do not attend indicates that gospel-related communication is too shallow for this generation.

We desperately need to be able to go deeper in our conversations about the spiritual life. The church would benefit from teaching members how to develop conversations around the gospel that are naturally authentic and highly relevant. I suggest two ways in a latter section which I call "Identification" and "Interpretation."

Addressing the Rise of the Irreligious

If recent generations are not influenced in radically different ways than previous generations have been influenced, then why do we have cultural and religious polarization growing so rapidly? Here is my theory. I see it as the continuation of trends that started with postmodernism. That means that the trends which began with postmodernism are now more intense, especially concerning how the gospel is heard and received. Clydesdale and Garces-Foley calls twenty-somethings "Practical Postmoderns" (Clydesdale & Garces-Foley, 2018, p. 163). Contemporary generations are not fundamentally different from the first postmodern generation.

If this continuity is correct, research should reveal that the authenticity valued by Generation X remains valued by younger generations and is necessary for them to be receptive to the gospel. This means that relational honesty and transparency are essential for reaching young adults today. Is this confirmed by research? Yes. Clydesdale and Garces-Foley write, "Authenticity came up repeatedly in our interviews with Evangelicals. They told us that their churches enable them to be themselves, without fear of judgement, something that they did not find possible at other churches. Alicia, a 24-year-old college student we met at New Life, also talked to us about authenticity. 'You can talk about the problems that you have and be honest, and you feel like it's a safe place for that...People can be real, and people are free to have their own opinions or struggle with whatever they are struggling with'" (Clydesdale & Garces-Foley, 2019, p. 122).

The continuation of postmodern values from one generation to another makes mutual understanding possible, but also brings the same difficulties. Twenty-somethings will distance themselves from institutions which are not perceived as authentic. "I am spiritual, but not religious," or "I do not believe in organized religion" are common sayings. Researcher Nancy Ammerman said, "Identifying as spiritual but not religious is evidence of an individual's desire to distance him or herself from the perceived evils perpetrated by organized religion, rather than descriptive of the individual's beliefs and practices." (Ammerman, 2013, p. 258–278). And she offers this assessment, "If [people] do not learn the language of spirituality in a religious community, it does not shape their way of being in the world. Spiritual, but not religious. Probably not" (Ammerman, 2014, para. 15).

I see a parallel to this sort of permanent spiritual distancing in what happened with outreach to the Jews in the first and second centuries. At first, the church was initially Jewish as Hebrews embraced Jesus as their Messiah (Green, 1970, p. 78–87). But as the Christian movement grew, Christianity was perceived as being anti-Jewish, slowing its growth (See Origen's argument against the Jewish interpretation of Isaiah 53, *Contra Celsum*, I:55). The church continued to grow but increasingly took on gentile values. I submit that a similar postmodern poisoning of the air has occurred today, and is now rather absorbed, undermining the church's influence.

When sitting down with Cru leaders at a central California university, I proposed this idea regarding cultural pre-conditioning, "A good proportion of young adults seem to have made emotive-level predeterminations about the Christian faith. From what they have gleaned of Christian voices and their associated beliefs, a barrier now precedes the gospel." The Cru staff immediately nodded in affirmation. They had seen it firsthand in the reactions of students they had tried to reach, reactions which indicated that the gospel message was viewed as powerless, if not intolerable.

The self-image of young people is a powerful force in forming their identity, which, in turn, influences their beliefs. If perceptions of Christians, Christianity, and church policies do not align with their notions of love, fairness, justice, equality, truth, and tolerance which they ascribe to themselves and their network of friends, why should they listen to the religious jargon of Christians or consider accepting an invitation to visit a church? Having already rejected the institutional form of Christianity, they believe they already know where pursuing further understanding of Christianity would lead.

How Research Informs Evangelism: Untangling Knots

These preconditioned responses to the gospel underline the insufficiency of a simple "Just go tell them about Jesus" approach. Because of their preconceived notion of Christianity, a close relationship with a genuine Christian or Christian group becomes crucial to the unraveling of misinformed conclusions. It was for this reason that Jesus emphasized love so much. With God, and the Spirit, there is always hope. But a deep, unobservable barrier exists for many young progressives.

Let me slightly modify the familiar biblical story of Jesus and the woman at the well (John 4). What if, hypothetically, the Jewish nation was primarily concerned, not with the Roman occupation, but with the loss of racial purity by intermarriage? It is clear that Jews did not routinely associate with Samaritans (John 4:9), but what if it was far more severe than that? What if the number one issue to the Jewish nation was racial purity and interactions with the Samaritan people were seen as the greatest threat? With all the religious fervor and rhetoric in the synagogues, the zeal against Samaria would flow into the streets stirring up crowds with chants of hatred.

If Jesus' visit to Jacob's well occurred in such a context, what would be different? The Samaritan woman would probably ask a different question. In the biblical account, she asks a theological question concerning the place of worship. But in this new version, she might ask a political or social leaning one such as, "Why do the Jewish people hate us so much?"

Is this not similar to what we observe with people outside the church who are conditioned to see Christians in a negative social and political light? I propose that, in the new scenario, though Jesus could have led the conversation in many different directions, the all-important spiritual conversation that took place that day might not have occurred. In that context, the hostility would be too great to overcome. In our reconstrued encounter between Jesus and the Samaritan woman, perhaps not even Jesus could have influenced her. It would certainly have been a different conversation. The Samaritan woman might not have been able to meaningfully dialogue with him, the contempt of her people being too painful. I had this exact kind of conversation on a New York radio program with a young caller named Jenny, where feelings of judgement and rejection from the church hindered her from understanding the love of God (Dr. Kevin interview, 2019).

Now, picture all those young progressives at colleges, on the streets protesting racial injustice, or in cities across the nation celebrating Biden's victory. Trump lost the 18-to-29-year-old vote by about 20 percent (Orr, 2020). Christians, including those who lean to the political right, should not view any of these people as beyond redemption. In a period of intense political polarization, Christians need a higher wisdom that prioritizes the gospel. I recall the day my pastor friend Mike Barnes described how he lost a friendship with his non-believing neighbor when he placed a Save Marriage initiative sign in his front lawn. He ended the story by declaring, "I will never do that again."

Analysis: The Efficacy of Evangelism

Because we are concerned about the most pluralistic generation in history, and because their resistance to institutional religion has biased them against the gospel and motivated them to leave church, we should ask, "How should we think about and do evangelism?"

First, we need to admit, as Clydesdale and Garces-Foley do, that understanding the religious attitudes of twenty-somethings does not necessarily show us how to reach them with the gospel. Likewise, Jean Twenge's proposals for saving *iGen* (Twenge, 2017, p. 289–313) do not provide any soteriological information. Research reveals what young people are predisposed to believe, but it does not describe how salvific faith develops from the multitude of starting points which characterize this generation. However, effective evangelism may not depend as much on generational distinctives as it is does on human nature. This is a simple point, but one that is important to make. Generational differences explain how people may be conditioned, but they do not change what it means to be human. So, the younger person has more in common with the older person than we may realize.

Second, Jesus's communication strategy focuses on human needs and storylines, not especially on generational distinctions. However, there are several references to age in the Bible. *The Prodigal Son* is a parable about a young man, but his age is not the focal point of the story, nor of humanity's need for a Savior as seen in the rest of Scripture. Modern market research into generational differences is valuable, but we should be careful not to overemphasize descriptive information of broad groups at the expense of responding to the exact needs of an individual. Rather than focusing on reaching a demographic, we should seek to reach unique individuals who happen to be a member of a specific generation.

Back to Jesus: A Dynamic Mission Approach
Jesus' method of evangelism is precisely what we need for the most pluralist generation for this one reason: His method is dynamic. It can reach anyone whatever their background and values may be. Christ's pattern of communication is powerful and can be summarized as: (1) Start where they are, (2) Read what they need, (3) Know where to take them. Christ's pattern does not reduce a person to a member of a demographic, but instead accurately assesses the unique needs and characteristics of the individual. (1) *Start where they are*: What does your twenty-something friend really think and feel about life and faith? (2) *Read what they need*: Become adept at seeing their needs and situations. Only then can you convey the gospel in a way that addresses those needs. (3) *Know where to take them*: This involves both accurately communicating the gospel and understanding the relational process and spiritual journey that are necessary so that they respond positively to the message.

An approach that takes into consideration the multitude of potential beliefs and backgrounds of the individual is likely to have a greater influence on younger generations than a more programmed approach. Here are three concepts that can be taught to members of churches to develop such an approach: (1) Identification: Personal connection, (2) Interpretation: Meaningful communication, and (3) Interception: Relational commitment.

Identification Through Story

Jean was in her 70s and a spiritual giant in my eyes. At a training class, she told of a conversation she had with a young woman who had shared about having marital troubles. As a Boomer, Jean saw this as an opportunity to speak of the power of Christ. Proud to shine as a light in the darkness, she quickly responded, "We are Christians, we don't have marital issues." My heart sank.

Such a response quickly diminished the likelihood of a positive response to the gospel. I tried to help Jean see things from a postmodern perspective, and how she could have replied more constructively. I pondered how difficult such a change of thinking would be for her. For her whole life she had been told that *if she really lived the Christian life* then others would see Jesus and want to know him.

As stated previously, postmodernism does not accept modernisms' idealistic beliefs about the communication of the gospel. The inability to relate, to connect, to help others see the realness of faith from the backdrop of their own human condition creates a massive gap between the believer and the unbeliever and an urgent need across the church. If we are to communicate more effectively with younger people, we must be more credible. To help Christians be more credible, I have taught a specific skill which involves using what I call "The Disclosure Window." This window is understood through adages such as "If they never see your darkness, they may never see his light," and "When you open up, you open a window to Christ."

Those who apply this skill have seen fruit. Scott Brennan describes the time with a college student he met through casual interactions at a Starbucks in Boston. As the relationship progressed, they had open and honest dialogues. During one conversation, the young adult revealed his struggle with same-sex attraction. Scott, in turn, told of the anguish he experienced from the words and abandonment of his father when he was twelve years old, and how the devastating wound wreaked havoc on his soul. In the video Scott recounts, "Right after I shared that, he began opening up, saying, 'You are talking about my life.'" As they continued the discussion, "Disclosure led to other disclosure. Through that I was able to allow him to share—to bring him to the place to come all the way out, and expose the fears, expose the sense of abandonment and shame. From there, it was so easy to direct him to Christ, saying: 'Is there anything holding you back?'" (Comer, 2015).

Having returned from visiting a church for four consecutive weeks, my 26-year-old mentioned that not once had the pastor shared anything related to his own life. He went on to inform me that he will not be going back. Pastors preaching sermons with a focus on abstract ideals do not connect emotionally with today's younger generations. Such pastors are more likely to have an effective ministry with Boomers and older seniors. Postmodern culture is hungry for something more transparent, reflecting the grittiness of human experience. Someone who has experienced life as they have experienced it is more likely to influence them.

Does this mean Christians need to reveal all of their sins, doubts, and fears to lead someone to Christ? Not always, but identification is a potent means to connect with young adults and to open the possibility for meaningful conversation.

Interpretation Through Story

Joshua Stock, president of Snowboarders for Christ (SFC), relayed how his young constituency understood that building relationships with unsaved friends was crucial, yet they saw few positive responses to the gospel. Many of their snowboarding friends lacked the motivation to follow Jesus (J.B. Stock, personal communication, July 19, 2012).

In Jesus' pattern of sharing the good news, he *reads what they need*, and then *interprets the good news* according to their situation. By "interpreting" so that the benefits and relevance of the gospel become clear, Jesus *motivated people to want to have faith.*

Dayna, one of our trainees, met with a nonreligious Japanese woman for lunch who shared that her husband had just confessed to having been unfaithful with scores of women. Practicing this skill of interpretation, she listened to this woman unload her sorrow, and asked herself. "What is her need? What does the gospel mean to her right now?" Sensing that the woman was overwhelmed by her feelings, Dayna saw a large planter close to their table, pointed to it, and said, "Maiko, you were not made to carry that planter, and you cannot carry this burden." She then shared about Jesus, the only One who could carry such a burden. Like Christ's "living water" metaphor, the massive planter became the image that led her to faith (Comer, 2018, p. 171).

A friend of mine who is a church leader in Kenya once made this observation, "In cities," where there is so much exposure to religions, "people are where they are regarding faith, not by chance, but by choice" (Z. Kingori, personal communication, August 10, 2013). What is the choice disbelieving urban Africans and young people all over the globe are making? *They are choosing to believe that a self-directed life is better than the life Christ offers them.* The church needs to be equipped to challenge that belief. We need Christians who grow close enough to young adults to help them understand what it means to have a relationship with Jesus. This is the power of interpretation.

For interpretation to occur, Christians should learn a process that leads to discovering how faith in Christ can respond to the particular needs of the unique individual:

Listening → Discovery → Interpretation → Communication

Again, this type of closeness and understanding rarely develops through social media; rather, it develops through a relationship, either through face-to-face communication or through video conferencing, in safe contexts that permit authentic sharing.

Interception Through Story

In a case study of a 4,000-member church in California, 36 believers were interviewed on sharing their faith; only two of them had an "ongoing" relationship with an unsaved person, making it highly unlikely that most of them would share their faith effectively. Though well-intentioned, church members who have no non-Christian friends rarely reach anyone. Even non-believers see this problem. Cru's research of 400 unbelievers from cities across America revealed that 84% had favorable views toward Jesus and were open to having conversations about him, most did not think

Christians would be willing to have a conversation with them because of the differences in their beliefs (Monaco, 2018).

To reach contemporary generations, we must develop relationships with those who do not believe as we do. Giving honor to others and creating a safe context for authentic conversations are essential virtues. Spiritual influence requires the right evangelistic approach. The "Philosophic Secularists" among twenty-somethings include skeptics and atheists. They can be reached if we help them to progress through the following:

Open to believing → Able to believe → Wanting to believe → Choosing to believe.

My experience of reaching two millennial skeptics indicates that they first need to be open to talk, for example, by meeting together every week. They then need sufficient information for the rationale to be able to believe; this may take months of weekly conversations. They then need to understand the benefits of the gospel so that they want to have faith; this comes through the interpretation of the benefits. Finally, they need to choose to follow Jesus, repenting and trusting him as their Lord and Savior.

Often, young adults reject the gospel because of a particular opinion or belief. Recently I watched a video of a millennial woman who, in all-earnestness, asked, "How can God save only Christians, while dismissing the people who have not yet heard or those who faithfully hold to other beliefs they have been taught?" Unfortunately, the apologist did not know how to address the core issue driving her inquiry. He needed to work the third part of Christ's pattern of communication, *Know where to take them.* Because he did not know how to do this, the woman eventually gave up and walked off.

There is only one way to respond to such a person whom I would call *the God accuser.* The details are in *Soul Whisperer* (Comer, 2013, p. 248–251), but my main point is that some young people will only be reached with sound, solid answers to their questions. Today, more than ever, we need church members who are relationally engaged but also specifically trained to reach those far from the gospel.

Twenty-Somethings and the Church Service

What about reaching young adults through church services? A strategy of attracting new people through programing, having the core group invite their friends, and encouraging belonging before belief has worked in the past. It is a simple, proven strategy, but its effectiveness has lessened dramatically with younger generations. A college minister invited 5 of his non-Christian friends to a church-sponsored event, but not one would attend. But were they willing to enter into a one-on-one conversation with him about their beliefs? Absolutely.

So, at church activities with young adults, make sure to promote a culture that is valued by this generation. The leaders should be relatable, authentic, up to date on current affairs, tech savvy, and socially conscious. These characteristics are useful for influencing those who are willing to come to church activities. But they do not always help to influence the rising number of younger people who will not come to a church activity. Church members with the necessary skills will need to gradually bring them into the community.

The proposed practices of identification, interpretation, and interception are essential for doing so. They enable Christians to influence today's youth. The church as a whole has failed to equip its members to be influencers of this generation. Mission concepts and practical skills are not widely taught, are not supported with viable structures, and are not valued by the church body. So we remain stuck in mission mediocrity. Ed Stetzer prophetically wrote, almost a generation ago, that postmoderns "need to be reached with the gospel of Jesus Christ, and the current pattern of church isn't reaching them" (Stetzer, 2003, p. 130).

Conclusion

Jesus critiqued his contemporaries, "How is it that you cannot interpret this present time?" (Luke 12:56). The church must read what is unfolding during this present time and be willing to change, otherwise it will lose what it has. A better missiological way lies before us. A time such as this, demands it.

References

Ammerman, N. T. (2013). Spiritual but not religious? Beyond binary choices in the study of religion," *Journal for the Scientific Study of Religion*, 52(2). 258–278.

Ammerman, N. T. (2014). The reality behind 'spiritual but not religious.' *Studying Congregations* (blog). http://studyingcongregations.org/blog/ask-the-expert-the-reality-behind-spiritual-but-not-religious

Barna Group. (2020). The State of the Church: What's on the Minds of America's Pastors. https://www.barna.com/research/whats_on_mind_americas_pastors/

Clydesdale T. and Garces-Foley, K. (2019). *The twenty-something soul: Understanding the religious and secular lives of American young adults*. Oxford University Press.

Comer, G. (2018). *ReMission: Rethinking how church leaders create movement*. Whitaker House.

Comer, G. (2013). *Soul whisperer: Why the church must change the way it views evangelism*, Wipf and Stock.

Comer, G. (2015). Real evangelism: Does honesty hurt the gospel? *Soul Whisperer Ministry*. https://www.youtube.com/watch?v=hqCoW3n9q4s

Comer, G. (2019). What's next for religion in 2019? [Radio broadcast] Dr. Kevin Show. *OM Times Radio*. https://www.facebook.com/watch/?v=2233136146953915

Frost, M. (2014). *Incarnate: The body of Christ in an age of disengagement*. InterVarsity Press.

Green, M. (1970). *Evangelism in the early church*. Eerdmans Publishing.

Green, E. (2020). The evangelical reckoning begins. *The Atlantic*.

Hybels, B. and L. (1995) *Rediscovering church: The story and vision of Willow Creek Community Church*, Zondervan.

Jones, V. (2020). "Election Day in America," CNN. November 7, 2020.

Kozey, R. (Oct 29, 2014) "Your Church on Mission: What's it Going to Take?" Southwest Church Planting Forum.

Loudwire, (2021). How grunge killed hair metal. https://loudwire.com/grunge-killed-ended-hair-metal/

Monaco, C. (2018). Cru's research reveals insights for gospel conversations. *The Send Institute*. https://www.sendinstitute.org/insights-gospel-conversations/

Noble, A. (2018). *Disruptive witness: Speaking truth in a distracted age*. InterVarsity Press.

Oden, T. (1995). The death of modernity and postmodern evangelical spirituality. Baker

Olson, L. (2019). 20 years, 700 victims: Southern Baptist sexual abuse spreads as leaders resist reforms. *Houston Chronicle*.

Origen, (c. 248/1980). *Contra Celsum*. Cambridge University Press.

Orr, G. (2020). Blame game erupts over Trump's decline in youth vote. *https://www.politico.com/news/2020/11/27/blame-game-erupts-over-trumps-decline-in-youth-vote-440811*

Pew Research (2014). 2014 Pew Religious Landscape Survey. http://www.pewresearch.org/fact-tank/2016/09/14/the-factors-driving-the-growth-of-religious-nones-in-the-s-s/ft_16-09-13_nones_growingshares/

Stetzer, E. (2003). *Planting new churches in a postmodern age.* B & H Publishers

Strobel, L. (2007). *Inside the mind of unchurched Harry and Mary: How to reach friends and family who avoid God and the church.* Harper-Collins.

Twenge, J. M. (2017) *iGen: Why today's super-connected kids are growing up less rebellious, more tolerant, less happy—and completely unprepared for adulthood.* Simon and Schuster.

Warren, R. Targeting Your Community for Evangelism. Purpose Driven Church Conference. https://bcbc.ca/wp-content/uploads/2020/02/Session-2-Targeting-your-Community-for-Evangelism.pdf

White, J. E. (2017). *Meet Generation Z.* Baker Books.

About the Author

Gary Comer is the founder of Soul Whisperer Ministry, an organization dedicated to helping churches develop missionally. After planting/pastoring two churches, Gary was hired by Sandals Church (a mega-sized younger, postmodern congregation in Southern California) as their outreach director. During that five-year stint, he also served as a church planting coach for the Christian Missionary Alliance and worked as an international mission trainer with Serve U International, while completing his doctorate at Talbot Theological Seminary, where he has served as an adjunct professor. *ReMission: Rethinking How Church Leaders Create Movement* is Gary's sixth book. His first book, *Soul Whisperer: Why the Church Must Change the Way It Views Evangelism,* is considered his signature work.

GREAT COMMISSION
RESEARCH JOURNAL
2021, Vol. 13(1) 61-85

My Pilgrimage in Church Growth

Charles Arn

The seven church board members eventually took their seats around the large circular table. The chairperson reached into his coat pocket, removed a stack of cards, and shuffled them as the conversation died down. Taking a card from the middle of the deck, he glanced at those seated around the table, then turned back to the card and read it aloud:

*"**Question:** The church picnic is coming up next month. In the past, the picnic has been for church members and their families. Someone has suggested that guests and neighbors be invited this year. The cost to the church will double for additional food and materials. Do you support the suggestion?"*

The chair paused momentarily. "All those in favor?" With no comments four of the members extended their arms and raised their thumbs skyward. "Those opposed?" The remaining three around the table turned their thumbs down as a sign of disagreement. The seven looked to the chair in anticipation as he read the bottom half of the card, *"**Answer:** This could be an excellent opportunity to meet friends and neighbors who might otherwise never visit the church. 'YES' — add 10 members; 'NO' — lose 5 members."* A cheer rose from the group, particularly the four whose correct votes had led to new members.

*"**Question #2"** said the chairman as he pulled out another card, *"The church high school department needs $2,000 for a retreat in the mountains this winter. The church has been asked*

for a donation. Should you vote for the gift?" The chairman turned to the group. "Those in favor?" This time the vote was a unanimous thumbs up as the board members confidently anticipated the additional members from an obviously correct answer.

"Answer:" read the chairperson, *"It would be important to clarify the purpose of the retreat. Will the event contribute to the outreach of the church? Or will it be only for high school kids who are already in the church? There is nothing wrong with a high school retreat. But all the departments in a church should be moving in the same direction. YES — add 2 members NO — add 5 members."* A murmur of disappointment rose from the group for not receiving the additional members.

And so the game continued for the next 15 minutes as participants slowly but surely learned how decisions they make as church leaders often affect the outreach and growth of a church.

The "Church Growth Eyes" card game was only one of a number of learning experiences I had the pleasure of creating over my years of involvement in the field of Church Growth. The name of this game came from Donald McGavran's expression *church growth eyes* meaning "A characteristic of Christians who have achieved an ability to see the possibilities of growth and to apply appropriate strategies to gain maximum results for Christ and His Church" (McGavran & Arn, 1977, p. 127).

But before I recollect my own pilgrimage in Church Growth, I want to point out that my footsteps closely follow those of my father, Win Arn, who many consider the "Father of the *American* Church Growth Movement." Win passed away in 2003 at the age of 83. Here is his story in his own words from the book *Ten Steps for Church Growth* (McGavran & Arn, 1977, pp.10-14):

> I came to Church Growth from a background in evangelism. As the director of a large evangelistic organization aimed primarily at winning youth, we had what we thought was an effective approach to a very winnable segment of society. A distinctive of the ministry was a youth rally where attendance of over 2000 per meeting was common. This rally included a variety of activities to attract youth, and

concluded with a message of salvation. Week after week, with few exceptions, 5 to 50 young people would come forward at the invitation to make a "decision." This appeared, at the time, to be very effective evangelism. Those who made "decisions" were counseled, given literature, and encouraged to attend a church. We kept in touch with them and followed their spiritual progress as much as possible.

While much good was accomplished in this ministry, I sensed problems. What happened to those who made "decisions"? Did they become growing, reproducing Christians? Did they become actively involved in a church? Some did, of course, and those individuals became the public illustrations used to validate this method of evangelism. But what about the others? What were the long-term results? What were the actual facts? I determined to find the answer.

I researched, collected data, interviewed, and analyzed until I had a body of significant facts. The results were startling! The "fruit that remained" was seriously lacking! The evangelistic effort included prayer, a fine staff, and proclamation of the gospel; yet much fruit seemed to fall to the ground, decay and die.

At this same time, I served as leader for an area-wide evangelistic crusade that brought to Portland, Oregon, a leading evangelist. He was preceded by a highly organized and efficient staff anticipating a two-week evangelistic campaign. Hundreds of prayer groups were formed. Billboards covered the city. Daily newspaper ads on television commercials foretold the event. Counselors were trained. Finances were raised. The crusade was held, decisions were made, and all acclaimed it a success.

When it was over and the team had gone, I again researched the "fruit". To my dismay, it was seriously lacking. What was wrong?

Friends gave me counsel: "Don't worry," said one, "if just one soul was saved it was worth it all." That didn't satisfy me. Another reassured me, "God keeps the records. Our job is to preach the Gospel." I couldn't fully accept that either. A third person said, "Some seeds fall on good ground; some fall on bad ground. You take what you get." But that wasn't enough truth for me. There had to be a better answer.

The problem, I soon discovered, extended beyond evangelistic crusades. The evangelistic dropout problem affected the church itself. The Home Mission Secretary of a large denomination described it within his own church community: "There is what we must describe as an obedience gap. Statistics show mortality rate of 75% of our new converts. Why is it that only one convert in four ever make it to the point of church membership?"

Struggling with the problem of the fruit that remains, I began to find answers. For example, I discovered that evangelistic efforts can be well advertised, financed, promoted, prayed for, and able to evoke decisions, yet be relatively fruitless if they are not a vital part of a local church ministry. In fact, the closer evangelism is integrated into a local church, the greater will be the "fruit that remains."

A second discovery was the need to change the goal from *decisions* to *disciples*. What a difference this made! A *decision* suggests a moment in time, a single event. A *disciple* suggests a way of life, incorporation into the body. The concept of *decision* has outlived its usefulness. The word is unbiblical and inadequate to describe the life commitment called for in Scripture.

A third discovery was that evangelism is more effective, not as a special once-a-year emphasis, but when it is built into the fabric of the church. When evangelism is an integral part of the continued program of every church, when Christians are meaningfully involved in outreach, two things happen: (1) those involved will grow and mature as they learn to witness, study the Word and learn to pray, and their numbers will grow; (2) there will be more "fruit that remains." When a new convert has found Christ through the efforts of the members of the local congregation, relationships have been established. A natural follow-up solves the problem that plagues most professional evangelist efforts — the "follow-up gap." The closer the sociological, psychological, relational bond between the new converts and established Christians in a local church, the greater the yield of fruit.

My pilgrimage to Church Growth really started in frustration and dissatisfaction with evangelistic methods I had seen and been a part of in America. My search led me to the local church. The church is God's plan for making disciples and for winning the world.

To acquire more expertise, I visited the School of World Mission and Church Growth at Fuller Theological Seminary. When I inquired about resources for American Church Growth, I found that Dr. Donald McGavran and C. Peter Wagner were team-teaching a course applying world principles of Church Growth to the American scene. I immediately enrolled. As I listened and learned, I realized here was the effective approach to evangelism for which I had been searching. In those hours, I experienced my third birth – "conversion" to Church Growth thinking.

As an American churchman, I saw the necessity of applying Church Growth concepts and insights to this nation. After my growth "conversion," I began to apply the gifts and abilities God had given me to help Church Growth thinking become known in America. The first step was to co-author a book with Dr. McGavran we called *How to Grow a Church*. As I write this [1978], the book is being used to introduce Church Growth throughout North America. Next came a 16mm film by the same name, followed by other films, articles, and seminars introducing and sharing the principles of Church Growth to America with the goal of increasing His Church.

I founded the Institute for American Church Growth as a "leap of faith." I resigned a comfortable denominational position and, without any visible means of support or even the assurance that America would receive Church Growth thinking, began the ministry. My strength was the knowledge that God wanted His Church to grow in America. That was enough! The Institute was organized for four purposes:

1) To motivate and encourage evangelism and Church Growth in America.
2) To enable individual churches to devise strategies and bold plans for growth.
3) To help pastors and lay people understand their growth problem and apply reproducible principles of growth.
4) To serve as a resource for the church-at-large in its growth efforts.

Today there is an exciting new ferment. God is doing a new thing in and through His Church. The principles and concepts of Church Growth are being used for effective evangelism in America and around the world. It is my hope and prayer that church leaders will consider and apply the insights of Church Growth thinking. Because, as Dr. McGavran is so fond of saying, and I of repeating: "It is God's will that His Church grow, that His lost children are found."

Getting Started in Church Growth

In 1973 I had enrolled in a master's program at the University of Southern California (USC) majoring in the field of Instructional Technology. At around the same time my father, Win Arn, had discovered the insights of Donald McGavran and started the Institute for American Church Growth to spread "Church Growth thinking" across North America. So, a number of the early Church Growth resources used by the Institute grew out of my class assignments at USC. For example, the "Church Growth Eyes" game was a final project for a class in simulation and gaming.

My introduction to Dr. McGavran was the result of a video production class I took at USC. Win also had an interest in media, having produced 28 films/videos, 5 seasons of Christian television shows, and a Christian radio program over the course of his career. One day Win mentioned the idea of producing a 16mm film featuring

Dr. McGavran and his Church Growth ideas. One question my dad wondered about was how this short little man with squinty eyes, graying goatee, and receding hairline (who bore a vague resemblance to Colonel Sanders) would come across on film. I suggested that we try filming McGavran for a short project related to my class at USC. Win asked Dr. McGavran if he would agree to a short video of him answering a few questions on Church Growth. "Don't expect much," Dr. McGavran responded, "but I'm happy to help." I borrowed the school's black and white reel-to-reel video recorder, and after a half hour of recording we played it back. It worked! McGavran had an engaging sparkle in his eye, conviction in his voice, and mastery of a topic that was brand new to the American Church. In the years following that first recording, Win Arn went on to produce several dozen films/videos that introduced "Church Growth Thinking" to literally tens of thousands of people in the greater Church. I remember Win saying one time that he liked making films because "...they go to places I will never be and speak to people I will never see." Another memory that comes to my mind was a time when Win showed Dr. McGavran the first cut of the 16mm film called "How to Grow a Church." It was a 28-minute film that did an excellent job of introducing viewers to McGavran and his Church Growth principles. After he had seen the film, McGavran turned to Win and said in characteristic humility, "Films make mountains out of mice."

How to Grow a Church: The Book and the Film

In the passage recounting his story, Win mentioned the book *How to Grow a Church*, the first book on American Church Growth that eventually sold over 250,000 copies. The format of the book was a dialogue between Arn and McGavran. As I reflect on this style, it was genius. Not only was the dialogue more engaging to readers (many of whom would be laypersons), it allowed Win to engage with Dr. McGavran on a variety of topics while still being somewhat of a novice in Church Growth. Here is a brief excerpt from Chapter One of *How to Grow a Church*. The topic of conversation is "possibilities for growth."

WIN ARN: So, if the potential is there, why is it that so many churches have not seen the possibilities and done something about it?

DONALD McGAVRAN: So many Christians have become accustomed to—preoccupied with—their own congregation. They like their own congregation. That's perfectly natural. They should. But unfortunately, the outsiders remain *outsiders*. There is no way of reaching these outsiders when a church is preoccupied with its own members. So, congregation after congregation is sealed off to itself, by its own language, its own culture, by its own degree of education, or wealth, or residence. The bridges to other segments of the population, across which Church Growth will occur, simply are not built (McGavran & Arn, 1973, p.3).

Many afternoons and evenings I would put a Wollensak reel-to-reel tape recorder in the trunk and my dad and I would drive to Dr. McGavran's house in Altadena, California. Mrs. McGavran always had a pot of tea prepared. He was always dressed in a suit and tie. I still remember my shock the first time I entered their living room and spotted a 30' python skin Dr. and Mrs. McGavran had brought back from their missionary work in India. On the opposite wall was a 10' tiger skin he said the locals had killed when the tiger was harassing their village. McGavran and Arn sat in the living room around a coffee table with only a few pages of notes and chatted about Church Growth. It was my job to set up the recorder and make sure the content was intelligible.

The content of the book was divided into chapters: 1) Possibilities for Growth, 2) Growing Churches of the New Testament, 3) Discovering Responsiveness, 4) Measuring Church Growth, 5) Leadership for Growing Churches, 6) Characteristics of Growing Churches, 7) First Church, 8) New Church, 9) Changing Church, 10) Suburban Church, and 11) Go and Grow. My mom's job, when we returned home, was to transcribe that evening's dialogue with an IBM Selectric typewriter. One of my mom's happiest days was when my dad brought a word processor home for her, since prior to that she had to retype the entire manuscript with each subsequent editing!

A year after its completion, *How to Grow a Church* was released. Billy Graham had written the Foreword, saying, "This is an exciting book which is at once both simple and profound. The authors challenge us to expect great things when God's work is done in God's way" (McGavran & Arn, 1973, pp.iii). McGavran and Arn went on to co-author three more books, all of which I had the privilege of editing. In fact, the third book (*Growth: A New Vision for the Sunday School*) I co-authored with Drs. McGavran and Arn. It was a book written on the 200th anniversary of the Sunday School (1980). In the text we sought to apply a number of Church Growth principles to the institution of the Sunday School whose national enrollment was declining even more dramatically than Protestant Church membership.

When we realized that the interview and dialogue technique used in the *How to Grow a Church* book seemed to work, we decided to try it on 16mm film. The genre of 16mm film, however, was a bit more challenging. To grab and hold viewers' attention for a half hour around a somewhat academic topic like Church Growth required more than just a talking head. We worked with a Christian film production company, Johnson/Nyquist, and identified the principles we wanted to highlight, the authorities we wanted to interview (featuring McGavran), and the case studies we wanted to use to illustrate Church Growth in action.

Gospel Films, Inc., an international Christian film distribution company, agreed to carry *How to Grow a Church* in their more than 40 local film libraries. This gave churches around the country access to the film and gave church members a chance to hear the message, "God wants your church to grow." I remember one scene in which Win Arn was discussing the topic of small groups with Dr. McGavran. Arn posed the question, "Can small groups help a church grow?" to which McGavran responded, "Small groups do promote friendship, love, harmony, mutual support. All those things are desirable. However, if the small group consists exclusively of people who are already Christians, exclusively of the existing members of the church, then it has very little meaning for the growth of the church. On the other hand, if the small group makes it a point to include within itself those who have not accepted

Christ, then the small group is one of the most effective ways of winning people to Christ."

This film was one of the most effective tools in the early days for introducing people to Church Growth thinking. A few years later, Win produced a sequel entitled "Reach Out and Grow" which included more authorities, case studies, and, of course, more of the little gray-haired, balding man telling viewers that "It is God's will that His Church grow, that His lost children are found."

The Institute for American Church Growth

When Win took the class at Fuller Seminary and discovered Church Growth, he was a regional executive with the Evangelical Covenant Church headquartered in Pasadena. With all that went with such work, he soon became frustrated with the "administrivia" that drew him away from his new passion of Church Growth. He determined to take a leap of faith and start a new ministry—the Institute for American Church Growth. As I look back on those early years, with a wife, four kids, house and car payments, and no identifiable means of income, Win had more faith than I could have mustered.

One of the early business items for the new company, after selecting a board (McGavran was chair, Peter Wagner was vice-chair), was to identify possible sources of funding to pay the bills. There were two sources of income, "products" and "services". The first category included books, films, posters, and a newsletter/magazine. The second included consulting with local and denominational church bodies, public speaking, and research. It sounded daunting. But we set out on the pilgrimage.

The first product the Institute produced was my little card game, "Church Growth Eyes." We also rented out copies of the film *How to Grow a Church* to churches. Gospel Light Publishers had printed and was distributing the book by the same name. To kick off the release of the book, Gospel Light asked Win and Dr. McGavran to present a leadership seminar. Attendance was greater than expected; it looked like several hundred from the photos I took. This experience gave us the idea that perhaps seminars could be another vehicle for spreading the insights of Church Growth. A few months later, Drs. Arn and McGavran led a second seminar in Portland, Oregon.

Coming home on the plane, we debriefed the experience and, out of that discussion, the "Basic Growth Seminar" was born.

Basic Growth Seminar

The resource of 16mm film (and later video tape) proved to be a tremendous tool to "go to places we'll never be, and speak to people we'll never see." At the same time, 30 minutes of watching a 16mm film was hardly enough to redirect the paradigms of church members from inward to outward. A 10-hour experience of thinking, laughing, sharing, and learning about Church Growth had greater potential.

The Basic Growth Seminar workbook cover read, "Envision your church exploding with life and vitality...reaching out and winning people...making disciples and responsible members...expanding new horizons...Christians enthusiastically involved in the ministry and outreach of your church...that's Church Growth!" Win and I worked together on designing the Friday night/Saturday seminar, creating a variety of teaching activities that kept participants (mostly laypersons) enjoying themselves and learning in the process. One of the teaching techniques I had learned at USC was to have participants take a quiz and then debrief it together. In the Basic Seminar, participants were divided into smaller groups and instructed to identify the correct answer to each of ten questions (with a "grand prize" going to the winning team). Once the groups had (hopefully) selected the right answers, the seminar leader would review each question along with an explanation and the correct answer. (The grand prize would turn out to be a free trip to the Hawaiian Islands, assuming the winning team could convince their pastor to cover the expenses!) Here are a few questions from the quiz. Can you get them right?

1. A local church has the best opportunity for growth when
   a. there are relatively few churches in the community
   b. there are many non-Christians in the community
   c. the members of the church have different demographic characteristics than the community
   d. there are many young people actively participating in the church and its activities

       e. it has established a "name for itself" in the community
2. Prior to dynamic church growth, it is most important to have an understanding
       a. of successful and unsuccessful methods used by other churches
       b. that it is God's will that His Church grow and His lost children are found
       c. of the church's theological position and doctrine
       d. of the community around the church
       e. of the church's growth goal and that members have an active part in achieving that goal
3. An early church in the New Testament was the first to cross the culture barrier of Jew and Gentile. The church was located in
       a. Laodicea
       b. Philippi
       c. Antioch
       d. Jerusalem
       e. Thessalonica

Another activity in the Basic Seminar was teaching participants new Church Growth terms such as "classes of leaders," "great commission goal," "non-growth excuses," and "removing the fog." Using a page in their seminar workbook titled Church Growth Glossary, participants were to write a super-sentence that included as many vocabulary words as possible. They then read the sentence to their neighbor who, if the sentence was exceptional, volunteered that person to read it to the group. The readings were inevitably followed by appreciative applause. It was a great learning experience... disguised as fun!

Still another learning experience was a session on "Growth-Restricting Obstacles" and "Non-Growth Excuses." Participants were first introduced to the definitions:

Growth-restricting obstacle — an internal or external barrier that keeps a church from growing.

Non-growth excuse — a rationalization of failure to grow, often used as justification for non-growth.

Then, on their own, seminar participants were to 1) list growth-restricting obstacles particularly related to their church and 2) list non-growth excuses also related to their church. Finally, they were to share and discuss their list with several people next to them. It was a great exercise in, what Donald McGavran used to call "removing the fog."

As the Church Growth movement became more and more widely known, Win and I began to ask the question, how do we *facilitate* the spread of these insights? After all, the Institute for American Church Growth was a relatively small organization, while there were thousands of churches and pastors that needed and wanted to grow. One idea was to invite denominational executives and pastors who had caught the vision of Church Growth to lead Basic Growth Seminars in their own network of churches. We packed a seminar leader's kit with films, overhead transparencies, and leader's notes and trained these men and women to present the seminar in their community. This idea worked to some extent. But it was my observation that there are certain communication skills and gifts that some have, and some do not. Win Arn had a special gift for leading a room full of people in the discovery and application of Church Growth that was hard to imitate.

Church Growth Films/Videos
Win felt that the greatest need in spreading Church Growth thinking was to communicate with laypeople. Of course, there is a place for training pastors, church planters, and regional and national church executives. But most pastors know that the hardest challenge they face in moving a church toward change and growth is *after* the leadership seminar that they and their staff have attended. The challenge is getting the members on board. Toward that end, we came upon the idea of creating a "typical" layperson that viewers (church members) could identify with on the journey of discovering Church Growth. Enter Chuck Bradley.

Chuck was a likable, somewhat gullible though dedicated

church member. (In reality, he was an excellent professional actor.) In his journey through 14 different 26-minute films Chuck helped viewers see that "If Chuck can do it, maybe I can do it, too." With the help of Johnson/Nyquist film productions, Win and I created a variety of ways and means by which Chuck learned something about Church Growth. We never used the term Church Growth, and we included Dr. McGavran in only one of these films. But Chuck brought many new insights and a "Church Growth conscience" (as Dr. McGavran used to call it) to tens of thousands of viewers. Titles in the series included:

- *But, I'm Just a Layman.* Chuck learns that growth and outreach is not just the pastor's job.
- *Discover Your Gifts.* Viewers discover the world of spiritual gifts as Chuck searches for his.
- *The Gift of Love.* Financial giving is not a duty, it's a privilege.
- *The Great Commission Sunday School.* What is the real purpose of the Sunday School?
- *The Possibility Sunday School.* Can a Sunday School reach new people and grow?
- *For the Love of Pete.* Chuck learns that God reaches people through relationships.
- *Who Cares About Love?* (Parts 1 & 2) The motive of reaching lost people is love; as is the message and the method.
- *A Matter of Urgency.* We all have priorities...what is yours and your church's?
- *The Ministers.* Chuck trades places with his twin brother (Rev. Bill Bradley) and discovers that pastors are not the only ministers.
- *In His Steps...What Would Jesus Do?* Chuck tries asking— and acting on—the question "What would Jesus do?"
- *See You Sunday.* An engaging film on assimilating newcomers into the life of the church.

Church Growth Magazine

One of the resources we developed in the early days of the Institute was a newsletter called *Church Growth: America.* Initially it was a simple 4-page, 2-color circular with a few odds and ends on Church Growth, along with several short articles. Ten years later, the publication had grown to a 24-page, color magazine with several in-depth articles. Lyle Schaller accepted my invitation to be a regular contributor. Win had a regular column. Cutting edge research was often included. One study on mass evangelism generated so much interest it was reported in *Time* magazine. As editor, I was proud to provide this resource to church leaders for a number of years.

Speaking about *Church Growth: America* reminds me of a "God moment" related to the magazine. Those familiar with Church Growth, and even those who are not, probably know the name Dr. Gary McIntosh. Gary is a prolific writer, with I-don't-know-how-many book titles to his credit. I later enjoyed co-authoring a book with Gary (*What Every Pastor Should Know*) that received *Outreach* magazine's Book of the Year award. A fun story about Gary's entry into the world of Church Growth comes through Win Arn's invitation to Gary, then a pastor of a small Baptist church in San Bernardino, California. *Christianity Today* had recently published an article proposing the importance of being a *faithful* pastor and congregation rather than being a *successful* one. The article did not sit well with me, as it seemed to be a non-growth excuse for any church leader who wanted to justify their ineffectiveness in evangelism and outreach. Gary had just submitted an article to *Church Growth: America* making a good case for the idea that faithfulness *brings* success. And if your church is not growing, it is usually a lame excuse to say that the reason is your faithfulness. I showed Win the article and we ran it the following month. This article put Gary on our radar, and before long we invited him to join the staff of the Institute. During his time with the Institute, Gary led numerous Basic Growth Seminars and conducted many church consultations. As a result of this association, Gary has (and continues to be) a prized friend in my life. His subsequent publishing, speaking, research, and leadership in the field is one of my proudest achievements!

The Master's Plan for Making Disciples

One of the ways Win and I produced new Church Growth resources was to read Dr. McGavran's writings and then identify the growth principles that could be contextualized for the American Church. One of McGavran's first books was *Bridges of God* (1955). In it, he introduces the powerful idea of "people movements." Here is how he opens the book: "A great deal of study has been devoted to Christian missions. We have come to know the answers to many questions about mission work. But what is perhaps the most important question of all still waits an answer. The question is: 'How do Peoples become Christian?'" (p.1).

The missionary McGavran continues, "This book asks how clans, tribes, castes, in short how Peoples become Christian. How do chain reactions in these strata of society begin? This is an inquiry which is of enormous concern to both younger and older churches as they carry out the great commission" (1955, p.1). McGavran uses the rest of the book to present his answer to this question. He writes of how *relationships within networks of people* are the bridges of God over which the Gospel travels. Whether it is within immediate family members, extended families, villages, or communities, the good news of the Christian faith moves and grows among common kinship, common friendships, and common associates.

This idea of People Movements led Win and me to research the ideas of "networks," "webs," and the Greek word *oikos* ("household"). Throughout the New Testament, the word "household" appears repeatedly in describing how the Gospel traveled and how people came to Christ (Acts 16:15, Acts 26:31, Luke 8:39, Luke 19:10, John 4:52, Acts 10:2,24, Acts 18:8, I Co. 1:16). This idea led to a book Win and I co-authored entitled *The Master's Plan for Making Disciples* (1982). We first printed the book ourselves and later it was later picked up and distributed by Baker Books. We partnered with Johnson/Nyquist Film Productions and created the 28-minute film, "For the Love of Pete," to illustrate the principles of identifying and reaching one's *oikos* of non-Christian friends, neighbors, and relatives.

While the book and film were in production, I was hard at work on a Master's Plan kit with a *Leader's Manual* for a layperson to lead a study. The kit also included a participant workbook, small group leader's guide, and additional material to discover and apply the *oikos* process in their church. One of my favorite examples of a church that took the *oikos* process seriously is High Desert Church in Victorville, California. Rev. Tom Mercer, pastor of this 12,000+ member church, writes about his *oikos* discovery in his own book, *8 to 15: The World is Smaller Than You Think:*

> Back in 1979, my senior pastor asked me to attend a seminar with him, one led by Dr. Win Arn. Until that time neither of us had heard much about the word "oikos," let alone the principle behind it. The church had hired me because the youth ministry needed a boost. (The first Bible Study I led had a grand total of four students.) It was at Dr. Arn's seminar that I was introduced to the basic principle of *oikos* that I'm going to share with you. Of course time and experience have refined its implementation. But it's efficiency lies in its pure simplicity.
>
> That seminar lit a fire under me! For the first time I began feeling like I could be a part of the great commission in a natural, authentic way. My pastor said "go for it." I felt like a youth pastor unleashed! Three years later the youth group was on the verge of outgrowing the church. Over 300 students had taken this simple idea seriously and had literally turned our community on its ear (2017, p.13).

Tom later became pastor of High Desert Church. He once told me, "Oikos is not *one* of the things we do, it's the *only thing* we do!" Of all the principles of Church Growth I have encountered in my 45 years of ministry in the field, I am convinced that the *oikos* principle is the most significant and holds the greatest potential for pivoting a declining church around toward new outreach and growth.

Church Growth Books

Over the years Win and I have written or co-authored a variety of books in the field of Church Growth:

- *How to Grow a Church* (Win Arn & Donald McGavran)
- *Ten Steps for Church Growth* (Win Arn & Donald McGavran)

- *Back to Basics in Church Growth* (Win Arn & Donald McGavran)
- *Growth: A New Vision for the Sunday School* (Charles Arn, Donald McGavran, Win Arn)
- *Who Cares About Love?* (Win Arn & Charles Arn)
- *The Master's Plan for Making Disciples* (Win Arn & Charles Arn)
- *The Pastor's Church Growth Handbook (Vol. I & 2)* (Win Arn)
- *The Church Growth Ratio Book* (Win Arn)
- *How to Start a New Service* (Charles Arn)
- *Side Door* (Charles Arn)
- *What Every Pastor Should Know* (Gary McIntosh & Charles Arn)

Other Church Growth Endeavors
In preparing this article, I dug into my old files and pulled out a 48-page catalog listing products and services available through the Institute for American Church Growth in 1983. Here are a few of the resources we had a part in developing.

Advanced Church Growth Seminar. A 4-day leadership training conference held in Pasadena, California, once a year. We averaged several hundred pastors and denominational executives, including a regular contingent of Korean pastors who would fly over from Seoul. A fun fact: A free scholarship to this Advanced Growth Seminar was the grand prize each year in a class at Southwestern Seminary for the student who read the most Church Growth books. The winner, one year, was Rick Warren.

Celebration of Friendship. A planning kit to organize and promote a "Friendship Sunday" where members were encouraged to bring a friend to church. Included in the kit were posters, bulletin covers, booklets, and more. The Church Growth principle behind the idea of bringing a friend was that 75% – 90% of all new believers came to faith through a friend, neighbor, or relative. "Our attendance was up by 150 people," said a pastor in Bradenton, Florida, after using this resource, "with a total of 750 present. We had fifty-one first-time visitors."

Lifestyle Evangelism Growth-Focus Module. A 10-month special emphasis which a church could sponsor, including a one-day lay seminar on lifestyle evangelism, The Master's Plan for Making Disciples resource kit, the Celebration of Friendship planning kit, and unlimited consultation with Institute staff throughout the year. Calling in Love. A comprehensive planning kit to lead a church in organizing and conducting a community-wide telemarking strategy promoting an upcoming outreach event in the church.

A Shepherd's Guide to Caring and Keeping. A planning and training kit to help a church implement a strategy for integrating new believers into the church. It included a 26-minute video "See You Sunday," teaching notes with overhead transparency slides, and participant handouts to lead six training sessions in the church.

Celebrating God's Family. A comprehensive guide for planning a party to celebrate the joy of Christian community in a church. Bulletin covers, "We are a family" booklets, posters, balloons, and more.

The Caring System. A planning kit for a church to organize a personal follow-up system for visitors and other new member prospects. The essence of this kit was later integrated into a computer database after personal computers came along.

Member Assimilation Growth-Focus Module. Materials and guidance for a church to conduct a 10-month emphasis on incorporating members into active involvement and using their spiritual gifts. It included materials for a local church lay seminar, a 16-mm film "See You Sunday," and a planning kit for a celebration of God's family.

Church Growth Library. Current books related to Church Growth.

Growing in Love. A 13-week adult study of steps to become a more loving person and church, particularly to those outside of the Christian community. It featured complete leader's notes, overhead transparency slides, student workbooks, a video "Who

Cares About Love?", and the book *Who Cares About Love* by Win and Charles Arn.

In His Steps...with Love. A planning kit for a church to sponsor a one-week emphasis where members ask the question, "What would Jesus do?" It included a task force planning guide, an application booklet, bulletin covers, 7-day diaries, and the 16mm film "In His Steps...".

Intentional Love 10-Month Growth-Focus Module. A church-wide emphasis on becoming a more loving church. This included a one-day local church seminar led by Institute staff, a 16mm film, member planning booklets, a taskforce leader's guide, and unlimited consultation with the Institute staff.

Celebration of Service. A taskforce planning guide to organize and promote a special Sunday celebration of lay ministry and service opportunities in the church.

Mobilizing Laity for Ministry. Material to lead a Ministry Discovery Seminar in a local church, including presentation notes and overhead transparency slides, participants' workbook, and a 16mm film "The Ministers."

10-Month Laity in Ministry Growth-Focus Module. An emphasis in a local church on the topic of lay ministry. It included a one-day church seminar led by the Institute staff, a planning kit to conduct a Celebration of Service Sunday, teaching materials to lead a Discover Your Ministry seminar, and unlimited consultation with the Institute staff.

Spiritual Gifts for Building the Body. A self- or group-study course exploring the spiritual gifts: what they are, how to discover them, and how to use them.

How to Build a Growing Sunday School. A six-week study for youth through senior adults. It included workbooks, a leader's guide, the videos "The Great Commission Sunday School" and "The Possibility Sunday School," the textbook *Growth: A New Vision for the Sunday School*, and a Sunday School growth game "Sunday School Growth Diagnostic Manual."

Exploring the Churches of the Revelation. Eight 5-minute films to complement a sermon series on the seven churches of Asia Minor.

Disciples in the Making. A 12-week adult study integrating six of the most popular "Chuck Bradley" videos. Complete leader's and student notes.

Sunday School Growth Seminar. A one-day seminar led in the local church or denominational region on the principles of Church Growth applied to the educational ministry of the church.

Sunday School Growth Game. A fun educational game that teaches Church Growth principles and their application for a church's Sunday School.

Love in Action 30-Month Church Growth Partnership. A long-term relationship between the Institute for American Church Growth and a regional group of churches. It included three on-site seminars, a variety of growth planning resources, Church Growth films, and unlimited consultation.

Church Growth Associate Training. Certification for pastors and denominational executives to present the seminars and training sessions developed by the Institute for American Church Growth.

Let the Church Grow. A 12-week adult study on Church Growth principles and how to apply them. It included complete leader's notes and student handouts.

A Church is Born. A 22-minute dramatic 16mm film featuring a church family who takes up the challenge to start a new church.

<u>Planned Parenthood for Churches</u>. A 26-minute documentary film on church planting strategy and why more churches should get involved in starting a new church.

<u>The Great Commission Church Planting Kit</u>. A planning kit for denominational and regional church bodies to plant seeds among local congregation leaders to consider planting a new church.

<u>Building the Church</u>. A series of six 5-minute films to be integrated into a sermon series on the early churches.

<u>Growth Opportunity Check-up</u>. A do-it-yourself research tool for a local church to gather data, analyze, and then present the findings to the congregation in a State of the Church day.

The Next Decade
We continued to seek out new ways to communicate Church Growth thinking for the next ten years or so. The Institute and Win Arn became fairly well-known among church leaders. My claim to fame was "Oh, you're Win Arn's son!" I remember the first time I spoke in front of a group of pastors ten years after I began my career in Church Growth research and writing (and only then because Win came down sick at the last minute). The thought of speaking as an authority on Church Growth to these men and women of God nearly paralyzed me, until Win said to me, "Remember, in the land of the blind, a one-eyed man is king." I used to recite that to myself for years each time I would stand up to speak.

Then one night I was at my mom and dad's place. Just before I was about to leave, my mom came into the living room and said, "I think something's wrong with Win." We went into their bedroom and Win was lying on top of the bed. He was conscious but speaking and moving very slowly. "I think we should call 911," my mom said, and we did. Win had had an aneurism. We spent the night at the Arcadia Methodist Hospital, and Win stayed in the hospital and later the rehab unit for several months. Thankfully, we had recently hired a Chief Operating Officer to help with the logistics of running the company. Win had once said to me, regarding his distaste for administrative details, "You start out with a vision, and wind up running a business."

Win's genius was his visionary thinking. He spoke of his "stomach aches" when a new "baby elephant" (i.e., a Church Growth idea) was about to be born. My genius, if one could call it that, was to turn his ideas into reality. It was a good combination of gifts and it was a joy working in that role.

To the COO's credit, we kept the Institute alive for several years. But as the Church Growth movement peaked, it became more and more apparent that times were changing. Win recovered to some degree from his aneurism. Interestingly he retained a good deal of his passion for finding and meeting needs. But his passion narrowed from "Church Growth" to "senior adults." His focus was not on taking care of old people, but on *reaching* unchurched older adults and applying the principles of Church Growth to this new target audience. The Institute promoted this new focus of helping churches develop a growth consciousness for reaching older adults. From the time Win recovered from his stoke to the time he retired ten years later, he and I became authorities in the field of growing an older adult ministry. (There was that one-eyed king again.) Just as Win had taken the principles of Church Growth and applied them to the American church, and later applied them to Sunday School, we began applying Church Growth principles to older adult ministry. This new focus included:

Books

- *Catch the Age Wave*
- *White Unto Harvest*
- *Live Long and Love It*
- *The New Senior*

Films/Video

- "How to Grow a Senior Adult Ministry"
- "Finding Your Ministry in the Age Wave"
- "New Life in the Age Wave
- "In His Steps in the Age Wave"

- "Finding the Right Friendships in the Age Wave"

Curriculum

- The Grand Way
- Starting a L.I.F.E. Club in Your Church

In Conclusion

While doing research for this article, I ran across a short essay Win Arn submitted to a contest sponsored by the U.S. Post Office. He wrote it several years after his aneurism and it is a good reminder to us of defining our priorities past, present, and future...

Travel Lightly by Win Arn

Have you ever seen a hearse pulling a U-Haul trailer? No, you can't take it with you!

It's so easy to become attached to things. But living abundantly does not mean accumulating extravagantly. The book of Ecclesiastes says: "To everything there is a season...a time to be born, a time to die...a time to keep and a time to cast aside..."

Healthy aging means entering the season of casting aside.

In the six years following a stroke I have learned much about what to keep and what to cast aside:

- *People are more important than things.* Given a choice of accumulating friends or accumulating objects, people win out every time.
- *Giving is more important than receiving.* The joy of helping others far exceeds the novelty of new acquisitions.
- *Productivity is more important than activity.* I am spending my time in ways that will leave something behind when I'm gone.
- *Health is more important than gratification.* It's easier for me to say "no" to a double banana split. Although it still takes effort!

So, what do I keep...and what do I toss? I keep what helps me practice these priorities, and helps me travel lightly.

I continued to oversee the work of the Institute for a few more years until it seemed prudent to close its doors. I was invited to serve on the faculty at Wesley Seminary (Marion, Indiana) as Visiting Professor of Outreach. I was encouraged, though not surprised, to see that even after the passing of McGavran, Arn, and other early pioneers, 21st century students continue to gain wisdom and insights from the Church Growth movement and Donald McGavran's mantra, "It's God's will that His Church grow, that His lost children are found."

References

Arm, C., McGavran, D., & Arn, W. (1980). *Growth: A new vision for Sunday school.* Church Growth Press.

Arn, W., & Arn. C. (1982). *The Master's plan for making disciples: Every Christian an effective witness through and enabling church.* Baker Books.

McGavran, D. (1955). *Bridges of God.* Friendship Press.

McGavran, D., & Arn, W. (1973). *How to grow a church.* Regal Books.

McGavran, D., & Arn, W. (1977). *Ten steps for church growth.* Harper & Row.

Mercer, T. (2017). *8 to 15: The world is smaller than you think.* Oikos Books.

GREAT COMMISSION
RESEARCH JOURNAL
2021, Vol. 13(1) 87-90

Book Review

A Testimony to All Peoples: Kingdom Movement Around the World

Dave Coles and Stan Parks, Ed.
345pp.

Reviewed by Gene Wilson, former church planter, now global catalyst with *ReachGlobal* and co-author with Craig Ott of *Global Church Planting—Biblical Principles and Best Practices for Multiplication,* Baker Academic 2011.

Jesus promised in Matthew 24:14 that "This gospel of the kingdom will be proclaimed in the whole world as a testimony to all *ethnē* (people groups), and then the end will come." The 24:14 vision is to see the gospel shared with every people group on earth in our generation. Editors Dave Coles and Stan Parks also lead the 24:14 Coalition. They have assembled an anthology of Church Planting Movement (CPM) articles and case studies to inform, inspire, and call the church to action.

The premise of this book is God is doing something unique in our day through kingdom movements with disciple making and church multiplication in their DNA. The editors have helped our understanding of CPMs through this compendium of articles and case studies by 37 authors from 10 different countries. Many of the authors are non-Western leaders of CPMs. The articles, most originally published in *Mission Frontiers,* are grouped in two parts: The first part centers on Jesus' Promise in Matt. 24:14 and describes how CPMs are accelerating the day of Christ's return. The second part reports how churches, agencies and individuals are responding to that appeal and describes how others can join in the 24:14 effort. The first part explores the nature of CPMs, including the dynamics, mind shifts, and commitments required for them to happen. Then case studies highlight some of the more notable movements in places as diverse as India, Haiti, and the Middle East. First-hand accounts are told by those directly involved in the movement or closely connected to it. Some movements have grown so quickly in size they appear exceptional and unattainable in other contexts. Others are presented in earlier stages of development when the growth can be tracked more readily. Indeed, the stories come from a broad array of contexts, including a few Western ones. Steve Addison, author of *Movements that Change the World* (IVP 2011), contributes a helpful historical perspective (Ch. 23) entitled "The Story of Movements and the Spread of the Gospel."

J. Snodgrass takes us back even further by quoting passages in the *Book of Acts* that document the powerful advance of the first gospel movement that traveled north and west from Jerusalem to Rome. He defines a biblical movement as "A dynamic advance of the gospel in the power of the Holy Spirit through multiple localities or peoples. This includes large in-gatherings of new believers, vibrant transforming faith, and multiplication of both disciples, churches and leaders."

Snodgrass and Stan Parks (Ch. 6) include qualitative dimensions of movements such as disciples growing in maturity, showing great faith, loving their neighbors and blessing those who persecute them. This takes us beyond the more familiar definition which stresses speed and scope: "a rapid multiplication of indigenous churches planting churches that sweeps through a people group or population segment" (Garrison 2004:21). The emphasis on rapid, explosive multiplication as a normative pattern is not found in Scripture. While desirable, they are not Biblical mandates or part of Jesus' Promise. Fortunately, most of the authors describe living out kingdom values along with numeric growth. The balance between transformation (the gospel working in depth) and multiplication (the gospel expanding in breadth) is indeed a positive development in CPM literature.

The second part of the book serves as a call to action. It presents several perspectives on how individuals, churches, and agencies can get involved in a CPM. Change is difficult. Leading an organization toward a CPM vision, strategy, and process can be costly. In Ch. 36, Charles D. Davis outlines five lessons the American Church is learning from CPMs. Each of these lessons calls churches to a shift in focus: (1) from come and see to go and tell evangelism, (2) from individual to group conversions, (3) from church growth to generations of reproducing churches, (4) from training that is highly specialized to training that is simple and reproducible, (5) from teaching for knowledge to obedience-based discipling.

Several examples present the challenges of moving from addition to multiplication. Aila Tasse, who leads a CPM network in East Africa, narrates his painful transition from merely adding churches to multiplying them through disciple-making movements (DMM). He was leading an agency that had about 48 missionaries, half of them bi-vocational, when he started making the shift in 2005. Thirteen missionaries, including two key leaders, left to join a denomination that offered better salaries and positions. For three years they spun their wheels. Aila was discouraged. But they stayed the course and eventually built a coalition of kingdom minded DMM practitioners. Now the leaders see themselves as catalysts rather than owners. From 2010 to 2019, their agency extended their reach to eleven countries and have seen 9,000 new churches planted.

This book is not technical or polemic. Indeed, this treasure trove of articles will be enjoyed by anyone who rejoices in the global spread of the gospel. Both students of global mission and practioners will appreciate the realism of its narratives, the diversity of its voices, and the internal coherence of its movement perspective. The appendices contain helpful definitions and clarifications. In his article Steve Smith communicates a sense of urgency and a "whatever it takes" commitment. Davis describes five lessons the American Church is learning from CPMs. This book is a must-read for anyone who has a CPM vision in the American post-Christian context.

I expect that skeptics who read it will have some of their questions answered but not all. For example: Is the definition of a church adequate? We are told (Ch. 10) that it must be biblical and reproducible and follow the pattern of Acts 2:42-47. However, a definition with baseline essentials would have been helpful. Can a church be considered planted without a group of spiritual leaders who meet the New Testament qualifications (Acts 6, Titus 1, and 1 Tim. 3)? The Scriptures are presented in several articles as a sufficient guard against heresy while the Epistles indicate that elders apt to teach and to correct are needed. The authors do not attempt to answer all our questions. Rather, they point to some amazing results and give glory to God.

Reading candid testimonials from all over the world gave me great joy. The FAQ section in the appendix was helpful in dispelling some myths and presenting a broader tent than I expected. I appreciated the recognition that many specialized ministries can contribute to movements and that not all workers are called to catalyze CPMs or embrace a CPM approach. Many in the early stages will resonate with Lee Wood's appeal (p. 137) to take care of the depth of their ministry so that God will take care of its breadth. In a nutshell, the book was informative, inspiring and challenging. If there is another edition, it would be helpful to include the names of the authors of each article in the Table of Contents and provide an index at the end.

GREAT COMMISSION
RESEARCH JOURNAL
2021, Vol. 13(1) 91-94

Book Review

Undivided Witness: Followers of Jesus, Community Development, and Least-Reached Communities

Edited by David Greenlee, Mark Galpin, and Paul Bendor-Samuel.
Oxford, United Kingdom: Regnum Book International, 2020
218 pages, Kindle.
USD $15.99

Reviewed by: David Bahena, *Doctor of Intercultural Studies student, Biola University.*

In *Undivided Witness* the authors explore the intersection between the Community Development (CD) and the Vibrant Communities of Jesus Followers (VCJF) that serve among the least reached in a conceptual and practical way (p. 14). This book joins the debate to overcome the dividing wall between evangelism and social action. The authors show us how a correct understanding of the nature of the mission and the Kingdom of God can lead us to bear undivided witness. The church is seen as an essential actor to achieve integral transformation.

In Chapter 1, Jonathan William lays the foundation for understanding the Kingdom of God and appreciating the relationship between CD and the rise of VCJF. The concept of the Kingdom of God is rooted in Scripture. Salvation points to Shalom, a "right, healed and restored relationship on multiple levels" (p. 39). This way, the VCFJ have a special place in the integral transformation since the church is the sign of the Kingdom of God and not the development agencies. In Chapter 2, David Greenlee explores how people enter the Kingdom of God and how this affects the way we do ministry. Later, in Chapter 3, Rizalina (Sally) Ababa helps us understand the integral mission is living our following of Jesus "in an undivided way in every aspect of life" (p. 61).

In Chapter 4, Gabriel Markus invites us to view our task in light of God's glory. There is no room to prioritize between proclamation and compassion; both are for the glory of God. In his reflection essay, Mark Galpin addresses the ethical dimension of evangelism in the context of CD. In Chapter 2, Greenlee warned us that we cannot ignore that CD workers are in a position of power. For Galpin, many mistakes are made by ignoring the context or having a limited understanding of God's kingdom. In Chapter 5, Holly Stewart helps us become aware of the spiritual conflict in the transformation process.

Robert Sluka invites us to see creation care as worship, witness, and obedience in Chapter 6. The Kingdom of God aims at the reconciliation and restoration of all creation. In Chapter 7, Mark Galpin argues for the VCJF. Real transformation occurs when experiencing freedom in Christ and is only possible if the vision of planting churches is included, since they contribute to discipleship to consolidate the transformation. Scott Breslin presents an excellent reflection, in Chapter 8, of how worker CDs are accountable to seven stakeholders: the affected people, the host Government, the donors, the international development sectors who have developed proper practice criteria, their organization, their conscience, and for the faith-based NGOs they consider God as the primary stakeholder.

A second reflection essay points to the issue of corruption. Martin Allaby mentioned the Bible denounces corruption, bribery, denial of justice, oppression, obtaining wealth by unjust means, and dishonesty (p. 147). In the least-reached context, the church is invited to bear a good witness, to pray, and to influence society and be ready to make a prophetic denunciation. In Chapter 9, Andrea C. Waldorf addresses seven shared principles of community development and church planting. Rosemary Hack, in Chapter 10, helps us understand who the least reached are. Some are hidden and separated not only from us but also from their society by hostility, danger, stigma, poverty, or complex webs of sin. They are less reached because the followers of Jesus do not live among them or have not seen them.

A third reflection essay is also dedicated to the theme of the least reached. It is an anonymous testimony that raises questions: Who are the least reached? Why are there least-reached people? Why are they not visible? Whose fault is it? The author warns us, "if we choose to ignore disability, illness, street children, refugees or migrants, we will continue to miss out on great foci of society" (p. 185). Paul Bendor-Samuels closes the book with a call to bear an undivided witness.

I want to highlight two significant contributions from this book. In each chapter there are stories from many communities. They challenge us to pay attention to our mission contexts so that they are the source of our theological and missional reflection. The second is the emphasis on trying to destroy the wall that divides evangelism and social action. For William, there is no distinction between verbal proclamation, physical help, or miraculous healing; all are expressions of the Kingdom. For Ababa, there is an unintegral approach when only the physical dimension is recognized or when one wants to share the gospel without recognizing the physical needs. For Markus, seeing the task from the perspective of God's glory does not leave space to prioritize between proclamation and compassion; both are important. Sadly, Waldorf mentioned, "our ministry and our lives could be testier to those around us when we live as whole people presenting a complete gospel" (p. 155). All this for the purpose of encouraging church planters to see CD not only as "a platform but as an integral feature of truly holistic mission" (p. 25). Likewise, it is a wake-up call so that the CD does not forget or reject the spiritual dimension in the transformation. Only then can it be possible to bear an undivided witness.

I would like to make two observations. The authors argue in favor of the VCJF in the integral transformation. While I recognize several authors repeat their calling to serve regardless of whether people accept Jesus or not, I wonder, should the Christian values of an NGO be evaluated only in the light of people's conversion? These questions lead me to the second observation. Galpin, in his reflection observes that, for some, an integral mission is to do social action and proclamation at the same time (p. 83). This creates tension in the people who serve in the context of suffering. In these contexts, verbal proclamation is easily coercive.

Overall, *Undivided Witness: Followers of Jesus, Community Development, and Least-Reached Communities* challenges us to rethink our concept of integral mission, and to bear a complete witness in the places that God has called us to serve. This book is a must-read for all missionaries and leaders of mission organizations.

Book Review

Misreading Scripture with Individualist Eyes: Patronage, Honor, and Shame in the Biblical World

E. Randolph Richards and Richard James
InterVarsity Press, 2020
281 pages

Reviewed by Brent H. Burdick, D. Min., Adjunct Professor of Missions, Gordon-Conwell Theological Seminary, Charlotte, North Carolina, and Director of the Lausanne Global Classroom.

The Bible was written from a collectivist cultural worldview that functioned under the societal structures of kinship, patronage, and honor/shame. If the Bible is to be understood as its original authors intended and as the people to whom it was written would have understood and interpreted it, these cultural values cannot be ignored. Unfortunately, as authors E. Randolph Richards and Richard James note in *Misreading Scripture with Individualist Eyes*, Westerners tend to read Scripture through the eyes of individualist culture and miss much of the deeper level meanings that went without being said in biblical collectivist culture. Thus, reading Scripture with individualist eyes can lead to misunderstandings, misinterpretations, and misapplications of the Bible.

Kinship, patronage, and honor/shame are as ingrained in collectivist societies as the concepts of rights, fairness, and freedom are in individualist ones. The book examines for example, how kinship for collectivists contributes to a totally different understanding of family relationships. While individualists see family as primarily composed of parents and children, collectivists understand family and community much more broadly and extended. Family and community also function inseparably from one's identity. The family and group from which one comes can never be ignored, discounted, or forgotten. This collectivist worldview has a huge impact on one's choices, life events, and actions. One of Richards and James' biblical examples of this is the story of Joseph (see pp. 11-12). Individualists read it as a story about personal or career success amid trying circumstances and make applications to life with that in mind, whereas the original collectivist readers of the story would see it as a story of the restoration of relationships in the family of Jacob. The resulting applications end up quite different when the story is read this way and are more faithful to the original intent of the author of Genesis.

Another collectivist social structure that individualists miss in Scripture is patronage, which the book discusses at length. Because collectivists identify themselves as integrally connected to a group, everyone in the group is responsible to some extent for others in the group. This creates relationships in the community where sharing and caring take on reciprocal expectations. The challenge, however, is to meet reciprocal expectations when there is an inequity of wealth and power in a relationship. How can a poor man ever expect to repay a rich man in his community for help given? The answer is patronage. In a patron-client relationship, the patron will provide opportunity, resources, or other benefits to the client in return for loyalty, respect, faithfulness, and gratitude. Biblically, the best example of this asymmetrical relationship is God to humans, but Scripture also shows this dynamic in human relationships. The story of Elisha and the wealthy Shunammite woman in 2 Kings (see p. 89-91), for example, shows how each brought to the other benefits which the other was not able to provide. Both persons were helped by the relationship, and the Lord worked in the situation to accomplish his purposes. This is not to say that collectivist patronage is better than individualism, just different, and the differences are important to be aware of. Jesus in fact critiqued some of the negative aspects of patronage and put limits on reciprocity so it would not be abused (See Matt. 5:38-42 discussed on p. 81-82). The point is to understand that patronage is part of the biblical social world and if individualists do not understand that it is there, much will be missed, and misunderstood.

Individualists also frequently miss in Scripture the dynamic of honor and shame found in collectivist cultures. Honor and shame are social tools used to reinforce community values and boundaries. Individualists on the other hand frequently use guilt to impose values. Honor and shame can be part of an individualist's perspective, but they are typically interpreted through individualist eyes rather than communally. Collective honor and shame are found all throughout Scripture. Honor is what people desired in the Ancient Near East and Greco-Roman worlds, whether they were a king, like Saul, or a simple fisherman, like Peter. The book examines various kinds of ascribed or earned honor, and even honor contests, which motivated and impacted collective human relationships and institutions. Shame on the other hand, which is not the opposite of honor in the Bible, was most often used biblically in a positive way to refocus or improve behavior in a group, resulting in transformation and growth for the person and community. Jesus, for example, used shame in Matt. 18:15-17 (See page 192). His teaching here uses gentle shaming to accomplish restoration to the community. Individualists, however, typically apply a negative use of shame. Individualist shame used with guilt ostracizes, but collective shame is restorative. Honor and shame clearly function differently in the biblical world. Understanding collective honor and shame will therefore lead to deeper biblical insights and applications to life.

The book is extremely insightful on two levels. First, it helps individualist students and teachers of Scripture develop an awareness and understanding of collective societal functioning in the interpretation of Scripture. This awareness would be very helpful for pastors and church leaders to minister more effectively to collectivist peoples amid an individualist culture. Second, the authors share fascinating personal experiences as they encounter modern-day collectivism cross-culturally. Individualist cross-cultural workers will therefore gain a greater awareness of collectivist worldviews as they read, which will help in doing more effective evangelism, discipleship, and ministry among collective cultures. The value of an individualist understanding biblical collectivism for Bible study, ministry, and cross-cultural engagement cannot be overstated.

If the book lacks anything, it is a discussion of how to tell when a collectivist worldview is in play in a Bible passage so misreading as an individualist can be avoided. Though there are many Bible dictionaries, encyclopedias, and commentaries available, these are often written from an individualist perspective. A listing of resources from collective cultures that highlight and explain collective cultural aspects in the Bible would be helpful. Still, this book will have a great impact in leading readers to a transformative awareness of the importance of seeing Scripture through collectivist eyes. It is a must-read for all individualists who read and teach the Bible and desire to interpret and apply Scripture more closely to its original collectivist context.

GREAT COMMISSION
RESEARCH JOURNAL
2021, Vol. 13(1) 99-102

Book Review

Honor, Shame, and the Gospel: Reframing Our Message and Ministry

Edited by Christopher Flanders and Werner Mischke
William Carey Publishing, 2020

Reviewed by Cameron D. Armstrong, author of *Listening Between the Lines: Thinking Missiologically about Romanian Culture* (2018). Cameron D. Armstrong (PhD, Biola University) serves with the International Mission Board in Bucharest, Romania, where he teaches at the Bucharest Baptist Theological Institute. Cameron's research interests include orality, theological education, and Romania.

The growth of "cancel culture" in North America depicts a world in which everyone is subject at all times to being honored or shamed. No longer a non-Western phenomenon, the opinion of the collective concerning an individual is now ubiquitous. The time for North American Christians to deeply consider honor and shame values has arrived.

In *Honor, Shame, and the Gospel,* Christopher Flanders and Werner Mischke bring together 16 authors with considerable missiological experience in various regions around the globe. The book is a result of the inaugural Honor and Shame Conference, which was held at Wheaton College in June 2017. Interestingly, Flanders and Mischke relate that the idea for the Honor and Shame Conference originally sparked out of an International Orality Network conference in 2014 on the intersections between orality, honor-shame, and theological education. Flanders and Mischke's goals for the book are twofold: assist current practice and "add energy" to further honor-shame dialogue (xxv).

Before moving into the actual chapters, Flanders and Mischke helpfully offer definitions of shame and honor. Whereas shame is "the feeling or condition of being unworthy or defective," honor is "the positive recognition of or by a group or individual based on some type of excellence or norm" (xviii). In other words, shame is a lingering sense of unworthiness; honor involves public recognition of excellence. According to Flanders and Mischke, the Bible displays God as intimately involved in addressing honor-shame, transforming our shame into honor, as well as calling for his people to honor him. An honor-shame dynamic pervades the Scriptures.

The book is divided into two sections. Section 1 considers honor-shame in "general contexts." The seven authors connect honor-shame with such issues as the glory of God, church history, and biblical interpretation. An impressive chapter by Jayson Georges quotes extensively from eight theologians across church history who used honor-shame language in their preaching, teaching, and writing. Another fascinating chapter on how Jesus was shamed in the Gospel of John, penned by E. Randolph Richards, notes, "Shame protects the boundaries of a group" (74).

Section 2 analyzes honor-shame in "various mission contexts." Eight chapters depict how missiologists are applying honor-shame research in global regions as diverse as San Francisco, Cambodia, Croatia, and the Muslim world. The honest reflections of authors regarding how they stumbled into honor-shame realizations is quite emotional. For example, Audrey Frank's chapter on ministering among Muslim women vividly portrays both their inherent shame and the power of the gospel to turn shame into honor. According to Frank, female honor is the "nucleus of all Muslim life" (199). Any attempt at gospel contextualization, then, must include honor-shame realities.

Honor, Shame, and the Gospel possesses at least three strengths. First, the honor-shame conversation is clearly driven by field-tested ministry. Far from being a closed, academic forum behind institutionalized walls, the authors of this volume are actively involved in real mission endeavors with real people. Second, the wide range of contexts from which the authors' experience comes is commendable. Honor-shame dynamics are shown to not only be something experienced by Asians or Muslims, but also by people in other regions, including North America. Third, the authors deeply engage the Bible. Especially in Section 1 of the book, the chapters by Stephen C. Hawthorne and Jackson Wu both illuminate the Bible's teaching on honor-shame and depict its necessity for the planting and equipping of local churches.

Concerning weaknesses, there are times when the authors contradict one another. One example includes the relationship between the concepts of honor and shame. In Steve Tracy's chapter on how honor-shame addresses abuse victims, he claims, "Shame is the opposite of honor" (103). Yet in an earlier chapter, E. Randolph Richards explicitly states the two are not opposites (74). Further, there seems to be a disagreement between authors concerning whether or not honor-shame is the only alternative to the Western value system of innocence-guilt. Tom Steffen, for example, posits other paradigms, such as power-fear and purity-pollution. Katie Rawson cites power-fear in her chapter on racial reconciliation. Yet these were the only mentions I found beyond honor-shame. While such contradictions indicate the honor-shame conversation is ongoing, a forewarning note in the introduction by Flanders and Mischke that the authors do not always agree could be helpful.

North American readers will be especially interested in the insights found in the chapters by Steve Hong and Katie Rawson. Based on his experience in urban San Francisco, Hong models how attention to honor and shame concepts informs his ministry among pluralists. For example, Hong invited his LGBTQ, atheist, and non-evangelical friends to his fiftieth birthday party, artfully chronicling his life story through photography, music, and dance. Hong maintains that Christian witness among pluralists can be innovatively powerful through vulnerability. Rawson's chapter on the use of honorific language in racial reconciliation provides a stimulating analysis for contemporary North American culture. Rawson's assertation that "personal and historical awareness" can lead to a "healthy shame" (177) of the realities of racism is a point well taken. The chapter also proves an introductory primer for honor- and shame-promoting behaviors, including the effects of such behaviors on intercultural relationships.

For producing a work of missiology available to both the academician and field worker, Flanders and Mischke are to be commended. This book details how honor-shame conversations are essential for developing and executing mission strategy for the 21st century. At the same time, the chapters humble and challenge readers with stories of how God transforms shame into honor for his glory.

GREAT COMMISSION
RESEARCH JOURNAL
2021, Vol. 13(1) 103-105

Book Review

The Learning Cycle: Insights for Faithful Teaching from Neuroscience and the Social Sciences

By Muriel I. Elmer and Duane H. Elmer
InterVarsity Press, 2020
223 pages
US$22.00

Reviewed by Nathaniel (Than) Veltman who currently serves as Mission Scholar in missiology and community development with United World Mission's Theological Education Initiative at the Ethiopian Graduate School of Theology in Addis Ababa, Ethiopia.

Muriel and Duane Elmer have served as both educators (Trinity International University and Trinity Evangelical Divinity School, respectively) and missionaries for many years. This diverse background uniquely situates them for understanding how students learn in both formal and informal settings. In *The Learning Cycle*, they draw on this deep well of experience to apply insights from neuroscience and the social sciences to teaching, and in particular to develop tools for discipleship in teaching the Bible.

Their core contention is that how our brains learn matters. The book begins with Duane's experience with a student named Moses in which he concludes that "Being told *what* to think did not help him know *how* to think nor *how* to solve problems" (2). While this insight is not particularly new, what is new is the recent growing body of support from neuroscience and social sciences for *The*

Learning Cycle first developed in Duane's doctoral research. *The Learning Cycle* presents a model of learning, rooted in neuroscience and social sciences, that integrates "the *cognitive* (thought, reason, logic), *affective* (emotion and feeling), and *psychomotor* (behavior) aspects of learning" (6-7). This integration holds important insights and implications for faithful teaching, particularly in the local church context of disciple-making.

The book is divided into seven sections, five of which focus on different key components of *The Learning Cycle.* These five sections link recall, the first component and the basis of learning, with additional key ingredients: appreciation, speculation, practice, and habit. In the first section, the discussion of appreciation draws on neuroscientific insights on emotion to show that "positive emotions draw us in and open the mind to learn; situations that surface negative emotions we will tend to avoid and close the door to processing information" (71). Experience, and the uncomfortable feeling of cognitive dissonance and the way our brains respond to it, is the focus of the second section. Although this feeling is uncomfortable, the authors highlight how "dissonance is a stimulus for further learning...*if* we are open to learning" (93). It is here that the authors note the disruptive nature of barriers to learning and offer tools and resources to overcome them. Cultural barriers, for example, are easily overlooked and should not be ignored. Becoming adept at identifying these potential barriers is an important endeavor for the teacher and overcoming them takes analysis and planning. The authors provide concrete "learning tasks" that can help address these barriers (120-126). Their suggestion for teaching dependency on Scripture and prayer is particularly helpful for making the learning process concrete and practical in moving beyond the cognitive level of knowledge to daily practice.

This leads to the third section in which the authors attend to transformative learning. It is here that the "priesthood of all believers as a learning community" is emphasized, in which "we are all contributors—necessary contributors for the body's growth" (142). This is further developed in their chapter on the importance of "making a clear connection between the truth and the practice of truth" (145). In creating this connection, teaching embraces how the brain learns and emphasizes those actions which enable deeper learning. This culminates in a final section on habit: teachers play an important role in encouraging the formation of good habits and replacing bad ones. Attention to habits produces a practical and tangible experience of teaching and learning in which the transformative power of the Bible takes root in peoples' lives.

Taken altogether, the model aims for learning and discipleship that embodies Christlikeness in character, integrity, and wisdom. The authors consistently draw on Scripture, including how Jesus himself employed cognitive dissonance in his teachings. The book is made deeply personal and relatable through Bible teaching stories and experiences that show the impact of the Learning Cycle in both formal and informal educational contexts.

While the authors do a good job of engaging with the neurosciences, one concern is the recent challenge leveled at neuroscience research and the field of psychology more generally: The vast majority of this research focuses on students who come from western, educated, industrialized, rich and democratic (WEIRD) contexts, a non-representative group of the world's population. This poses a potentially severe limitation on neuroscience research for cross-cultural application. The challenge is particularly notable for the chapter on emotion, which draws on somewhat dated research. This is not so much a critique as much as a caution in direct application to non-western contexts and among minority groups in the US.

This book is aimed at Christian theological educators in higher education, including administrators. However, reflective of the authors' commitment to the local church and Christian education, anyone involved in teaching, guiding, or educating of any kind, including pastors and Sunday School teachers, will benefit from the insights into learning and the various tools presented in this book. It will serve as a helpful resource for discipleship among high schoolers, college students, and adults of all ages.

GCRN 2021 Virtual Conference

Pandemic-Related Innovations in Churches

June 11, 2021
10am to 2pm CT

Registration is free:
https://www.greatcommissionresearch.com/conference

Half-Day Webinar

Zoom links will be sent to those registered.
All times are Central Time.

10:00-10:10	**Introduction**
10:10-10:35	**Plenary Speaker 1: York Moore, National Evangelist, InterVarsity**
10:35-11:00	**Plenary Speaker 2: Doug Paul, Innovation Strategist, Catapult.**
11-11:10	**Break**
11:10-11:30	**Breakout discussions**
11:30-Noon	**Q&A with the two plenary speakers**
Noon-1:00	**Break for lunch**
1:00-1:40	**Breakout sessions covering specific innovations**
1:40-2:00	**President's final message**

CALL FOR SUBMISSIONS

Pandemic-Related Innovations in Churches
Sponsored by the Great Commission Research Network and Knox Fellowship

Purpose:
To compile and disseminate outstanding innovations in evangelism and church planting developed during the 2020-21 pandemic and lock-down.

Submissions (Due April 30):
Submissions should be between 1200 and 2400 words, describing one specific innovation that maintained or increased effectiveness in evangelism and church planting during the pandemic. These innovations may be, but are not necessarily, related to technology. Since these innovations share a common background of the COVID-19 pandemic, no background information concerning the pandemic needs to be included in the submission. However, local specifics, such as stay-at-home orders mandated by state, county, or city authorities, which are relevant to the innovation should be explained. Innovations that require more than 2400 words should be split up into smaller innovations. There is no limit to the number of submissions an individual or church can make. Submissions should be emailed by April 30, 2021, to David Dunaetz, editor of the *Great Commission Research Journal*: ddunaetz@apu.edu

Publication and Awards:
The authors of the top 4 innovations will receive a monetary prize of $500 (to be shared in the case of multiple-author submissions). The most valuable innovations will be published in a forthcoming issue of the *Great Commission Research Journal*. Selected authors will also be given an opportunity to present their innovations at the Great Commission Research Network's online conference on June 11, 2021. If there are a sufficient number of valuable innovations, they will be published in a book.

GREAT COMMISSION RESEARCH NETWORK

(formerly: The American Society for Church Growth)

OFFICERS

President:
Dr. Jay Moon
Professor of Church Planting and Evangelism
Asbury Theological Seminary
Email: jay.moon@asburyseminary.edu

First Vice President:
Dr. Winfield Bevins
Director, Asbury Theological Seminary Church
Planting Initiative
Email: winfield.bevins@asburyseminary.edu

Second Vice President:
Dr. Brad Ransom
Chief Training Officer
Director of Church Planting
Free Will Baptist North American Ministries
Email: brad@nafwb.org

Treasurer:
Ben Penfold
Chief Executive Officer
Penfold & Company

GREAT COMMISSION RESEARCH NETWORK
greatcommissionresearch.com

MEMBERSHIP

What is the Great Commission Research Network?
The Great Commission Research Network (GCRN) is a worldwide and professional association of Christian leaders whose ministry activities have been influenced by the basic and key principles of church growth as originally developed by the late Donald McGavran. Founded by renowned missiologists George G. Hunter III and C. Peter Wagner, the GCRN has expanded into an affiliation of church leaders who share research, examine case studies, dialogue with cutting-edge leaders, and network with fellow church professionals who are committed to helping local churches expand the kingdom through disciple-making.

Who Can Join the GCRN?
GCRN membership is open to all who wish a professional affiliation with colleagues in the field. The membership includes theoreticians, such as professors of evangelism and missions, and practitioners, such as pastors, denominational executives, parachurch leaders, church planters, researchers, mission leaders, and consultants. Some members specialize in domestic or mono-cultural church growth, while others are cross-culturally oriented.

Why Join the GCRN?
The GCRN provides a forum for maximum interaction among leaders, ministries, and resources on the cutting edge of Great Commission research. The annual conference of the GCRN (typically held in March each year) offers the opportunity for research updates and information on new resources and developments, as well as fellowship and encouragement from colleagues in the field of church growth. Membership in the GCRN includes a subscription to the *Great Commission Research Journal* and a discount for the annual conference.

How Do I Join the GCRN?

For further information on membership and the annual conference, please visit greatcommissionresearch.com.

Membership Fees

- One-year regular membership (inside or outside USA) - $59
- One-year student/senior adult membership (inside or outside USA) - $39
- Three-year regular membership (inside or outside USA) - $177
- Three-year senior membership (inside or outside USA) - $117
- Membership includes a subscription to the *Great Commission Research Journal* which is in the process of transitioning to an electronic format.

GREAT COMMISSION RESEARCH NETWORK
AWARDS

Donald A. McGavran Award for Outstanding Leadership in Great Commission Research

Normally once each year, the GCRN gives this award to an individual for exemplary scholarship, intellect, and leadership in the research and dissemination of the principles of effective disciple-making as described by Donald A. McGavran. The award recipients to date:

Win Arn	1989	Rick Warren	2004
C. Peter Wagner	1990	Charles Arn	2005
Carl F. George	1991	John Vaughan	2006
Wilbert S. McKinley	1992	Waldo Werning	2006
Robert Logan	1993	Bob Whitesel	2007
Bill Sullivan	1994	Bill Easum	2009
Elmer Towns	1994	Thom S. Rainer	2010
Flavil R. Yeakley Jr.	1995	Ed Stetzer	2012
George G. Hunter III	1996	Nelson Searcy	2013
Eddie Gibbs	1997	J. D. Payne	2014
Gary L. McIntosh	1998	Alan McMahan	2015
Kent R. Hunter	1999	Steve Wilkes	2016
R. Daniel Reeves	2000	Art McPhee	2016
Ray Ellis	2002	Mike Morris	2017
John Ellas	2003	Bill Day	2019

Win Arn Lifetime Achievement Award in Great Commission Research

This award is given to a person who has excelled in the field of American church growth over a long period of time. The award recipients to date:

Eddie Gibbs	2011	Gary McIntosh	2015
Elmer Towns	2012	Kent R. Hunter	2017
George G. Hunter III	2013	Carl George	2019
John Vaughan	2014		

American Society for Church Growth/GCRN Past Presidents

C. Peter Wagner	1986	Ray W. Ellis	1999-00
George G. Hunter III	1987	Charles Van Engen	2001-02
Kent R. Hunter	1988	Charles Arn	2003-04
Elmer Towns	1989	Alan McMahan	2005-06
Eddie Gibbs	1990	Eric Baumgartner	2007-08
Bill Sullivan	1991	Bob Whitesel	2009-12
Carl F. George	1992	Steve Wilkes	2013-14
Flavil Yeakley Jr.	1993	Mike Morris	2015-16
John Vaughan	1994	James Cho	2017-18
Gary L. McIntosh	1995-96	Gordon Penfold	2019-20
R. Daniel Reeves	1997-98		

GREAT COMMISSION RESEARCH NETWORK

SUBMISSIONS

The *Great Commission Research Journal* publishes both peer-reviewed articles reporting original research and reviews of recent books relevant to evangelism and disciple making.

The scope of the journal includes research focusing on evangelism, church planting, church growth, spiritual formation, church renewal, worship, or missions. Articles come from both members and non-members of the Great Commission Research Network and are generally unsolicited submissions, which are welcomed and will be considered for peer-review. There is no charge for submission or publication.

ARTICLES

All submissions should be emailed to the editor, David R. Dunaetz at ddunaetz@apu.edu.

Peer Review Process

Only the highest quality submissions presenting original research within the scope of the journal will be chosen for publication. To ensure this, all articles will go through a peer review process. Articles deemed by the editor to have potential for publication will be sent to reviewers (members of the editorial board or other reviewers with the needed expertise) for their recommendation. Upon receiving the reviewers' recommendations, the author will be notified that the submission was either rejected, that the submission has potential but needs to be significantly revised and resubmitted, that the submission is conditionally accepted if the noted issues are addressed, or that the submission is accepted unconditionally.

Format

Papers should be APA formatted according to the 7th edition of the Publication Manual of the American Psychological Association. Submissions should include a cover page, be double-spaced in Times New Roman, and be between 3,000 and 7,000 words (approximately 10-22 pages) in .docx format. Contact the editor for exceptions to this word count.

In-text references should be in the form (Smith, 2020) or (Smith, 2020, p.100). At the end of the article should be a References section. No footnotes should be used. Minimize the use of endnotes. If endnotes are necessary, more than two or three are strongly discouraged; rather than using Microsoft Word's endnote tool, place them manually before the References section.

Include an abstract of approximately 100-150 words at the beginning of your text.

After the References section, include a short biography (approximately 30 words) for each author.

BOOK REVIEWS

The purpose of our book reviews is to direct the reader to books that contribute to the broader disciple making endeavors of the church. The review (500-2000 words) is to help potential readers understand how the book will contribute to their ministry, especially those in North America or which have a large cross-cultural base. The review should consist of a summary of the contents, an evaluation of the book, and a description of how the book is applicable to practitioners.

Before submitting a book review, please contact the book review editor Dr. Kelton Hinton (khinton247@gmail.com) to either propose a book to be reviewed or to ask if there is a book that needs to be reviewed.

COPYRIGHT

CONTACT INFORMATION

To submit an article or for general questions, contact:
Dr. David Dunaetz, ddunaetz@apu.edu

For questions about book reviews, contact:
Dr. Kelton Hinton, khinton247@gmail.com

Made in the USA
Middletown, DE
01 May 2021

38172864R00066